Incredible
Kratu

Incredible
Kratu

The happy-go-lucky rescue dog who
changed his owner's life

Tess Eagle Swan
& Lynne Barrett-Lee

JB

Published by John Blake Publishing,
an imprint of Bonnier Books UK
4th Floor, Victoria House
Bloomsbury Square
London, WC1B 4DA

Owned by Bonnier Books
Sveavägen 56, Stockholm, Sweden

www.facebook.com/johnblakebooks
twitter.com/jblakebooks

Hardback: 978-1-78946-516-7
Ebook: 978-1-78946-515-0
Audio: 978-1-78946-589-1

Design by www.envydesign.co.uk

Printed and bound in Great Britain by Clays Ltd, Elcograf S.p.A

1 3 5 7 9 10 8 6 4 2

Every reasonable effort has been made to trace copyright-holders of material
reproduced in this book, but if any have been inadvertently overlooked the
publishers would be glad to hear from them.

John Blake Publishing is an imprint of Bonnier Books UK
www.bonnierbooks.co.uk

Gautama Buddha once said, 'When you come upon a path that brings benefit and happiness to all, follow this course as the moon journeys through the stars.' I especially value this saying and with this in mind, this book is dedicated with much love to Tutty, whose son Kratu guided me on to that path. My path of heart.

Contents

Foreword
by Peter Egan

I f you are reading this foreword, I hope you have either bought this remarkable book or are about to do so. I can assure you that you won't regret it. *Incredible Kratu* is a story of courage, bravery and above all, incredible and inspiring companionship. I have had the great pleasure of meeting both Tess and Kratu on a number of occasions, both here in the UK in the House of Commons and in the European Parliament. Kratu's appearance at the EU was a first and a riveting moment for those taking part in my presentation regarding the horrible situation facing stray dogs in Romania and throughout Eastern Europe.

Kratu is a remarkable companion, which, when you consider the life that Tess rescued him from, is a testament to the description 'companion animal' and this wonderful dog's great heart. Everything about his life before rescue was dismal and deeply depressing. You will journey with Tess through her own life, also full of challenge and heartbreak, until she meets this remarkable dog.

It is difficult to determine whether Tess saved Kratu or whether

Kratu saved Tess. Either way, their individual stories are remarkable, heartbreaking and inspiring. The most important outcome is that they found each other. This is clearly a meeting of two souls who were destined to intertwine and in so doing save and strengthen both their lives together and inspire others about the meaning of kindness, love and compassion.

Enjoy this journey ... You are in for a treat.

Peter Egan
Television and film actor
Advocate of animal rights
UK ambassador for Animals Asia Foundation
Patron of many charities
June 2021

CHAPTER 1

Wish Upon a Star

Just outside Cluj-Napoca, Transylvania, December 2013

Tutty was exhausted and about to give birth to another litter of puppies. She had a litter every season and invariably she lost them, either to disease (they were never vaccinated and many were just left to wander off and starve) or, more usually, because they were sold or given away to local people in exchange for whatever human things her owners needed.

Just one of Tutty's last litter remained. From the half-derelict outbuildings where she'd crawled under pallets to give birth, she could see him across the yard, the white patches on his coat bright in the moonlight. Her handsome boy, such a gentle soul, chained up as a guard dog, his sad eyes telling the story of his miserable existence; a fresh open wound was congealing on the top of his head, where, unable to escape, he'd been beaten with a piece of wood. That was how it went. The men would drink and when drunk, they would lash out at the women, the children, the dogs.

The Roma camp that was Tutty's home was on the edge of open country and well away from prying eyes. There was no water, no electricity and, for the dogs, little food; they mostly scavenged among the rubbish strewn all around and such water as they had came only when it rained.

In this world, the only one Tutty knew, dogs were treated as objects. In the eyes of their owners, they didn't have feelings; they were simply there to do a job of work or, in Tutty's case, used as a production line. As such, they never saw a vet, were never neutered, never microchipped and if four out of five puppies died from parvo or distemper – two highly contagious and potentially fatal viral diseases – or, as might happen now, from the relentless sub-zero temperatures, it was treated as natural selection. It didn't matter; there would always be more coming along.

Making it to adulthood was not guaranteed either. Adult dogs died from untreated wounds, starvation and disease, or lost their lives as a result of being beaten. Few survived to any age and those that did were often battered and broken. Tutty's body was a testament to the life she'd so far lived and the beatings endured from the old man who owned her. Her teeth were so bad that most of them had rotted away now and she walked with a limp after being hit by a tractor, the broken bones having subsequently not set right. Her ribs had nothing on them other than matted filthy fur, while her long saggy teats, which hung down almost to the ground, were now filling up in readiness for the births.

Whimpering, Tutty gave herself over to the pain, settled as best she could on the ice-hardened ground and raised her gaze to the stars, as if wishing for a miracle. She had never known a kind word, felt a gentle touch or a full belly. Had never experienced what it felt like to be free of pain and fear. But her wish was not for herself – it was, as always, for her soon-to-be-born puppies. That their lives, by that miracle, would be better than hers was.

The air was cold, the sky clear, the stars shining down brightly.

'Help my puppies,' she seemed to implore. 'Keep them safe.'

Two thousand miles away, that night, beneath the same stars, another wounded soul was raising her gaze to the constellations. A kindred spirit, whose wish for help was every bit as heartfelt, because she too knew what it felt like to be constantly in pain, to have been badly hurt by humans, to have to fight just to survive. To feel she didn't have enough strength to go on.

'Please help me,' she implored. 'I cannot bear to go on. Living just hurts too much. I am so tired of life. Please help me.'

That wounded soul was mine.

I often struggle with life, because I've struggled *all* my life. In myriad ways too, and for the most part *because* of life, because I just seemed to not be able to understand it. That night had been a low point. That whole winter hard. I was glad it was finally over.

But now, four months later, on a chilly April morning, I was struggling again and on multiple fronts. Some were as familiar as breathing (other people, being outside my comfort zone, other people), others, mostly specific, almost all self-inflicted, and directly related to the mission I was on, which was to go and collect a Romanian rescue puppy from a horse yard.

As usual, I was struggling mostly with my nerves. And by now I was, of course, extremely nervous. Probably because I'd been up half the night for several nights in a row now, checking and double-checking all the screenshots of the vital paperwork, then following the puppy's journey all the way from Cluj-Napoca in Transylvania to Ingatestone in Essex, using the tracker app for the transporter van he was coming on.

He had in fact almost missed the van because my friend Celia – who had been fostering him and was reliant on someone else to drive her – had been so late getting to the pickup point. I'd had a call from the transport people to tell me that if she didn't arrive soon then they were going to leave without her, causing me to almost spontaneously combust. Happily, I didn't (quite) and thankfully she got there, but not before we had a frank exchange of views over the phone about what constituted a sensible time to set off. (And poor Celia, having borne the brunt of me being pissed off, then had to suffer being pissed *on* – by my puppy. Shortly before arriving, he decided to relieve himself on her lap.) But even when I knew he had crossed the Channel safely there was still the anxiety about him arriving at Dover, where I knew a single misstep could see him denied entry into the UK, given the multiple customs hoops that still needed jumping through.

My own journey had been shorter; just the sixty or so miles from Witchford in Cambridgeshire, where I lived, which had taken just over an hour. I'd spent most of it trying to persuade myself to calm down. To remind myself that there was nothing to be scared of; that I was just another person picking up a rescue puppy and it wasn't like I hadn't done so before.

It hadn't worked. Nothing tended to. The intrusive thoughts were just too strong sometimes. One such thought and I'd be off, thoughts firing at me like a machine gun, feeding the fear and trying to persuade me why I should not be doing this. I'd be picturing horrific road accidents – the screech of brakes, the thunk of metal upon metal, scenes of gore and devastation, everyone dying, the mournful wail of sirens. It wasn't so much agoraphobia as extreme anxiety that would sneak up on me and set my heart banging against my ribcage any time I left the confines of my home – my comfort zone. And going to a place I didn't know, to meet people I didn't know, was a long way out there in the discomfort zone.

But the thought of the puppy – *my* puppy – spurred me on. Because if I didn't go and fetch him, what would become of him? I'd spent the last three months following and orchestrating his progress on a daily basis since I'd had the news from Celia, who lived in Cluj-Napoca, that she'd found him. We went back a way, Celia and I. Having initially connected due to our interest in dogs and horses, we soon realised we were like-minded souls. Since we'd first met on Facebook the previous year we'd rescued and rehomed over twenty dogs together, mostly puppies but some adult dogs too. But this one was different: I had asked Celia to find him for *me*. And from the moment I'd seen the first photographs of him and his dejected broken mother, something had broken in me too.

I think it was another piece of my heart.

I just saw something in his mother, whose name I didn't know then but whom I'd decided to call Beauty. I sensed a broken kindred spirit. A sentient being who, like me, must feel so, so sad and alone. No one had helped me, but my goodness, I was going to help her. It was almost as if a fire had been ignited inside me, a fierce, powerful force. I had never wanted to stand up for someone else the way I did for her. That connection – of being broken, in pain and so dejected – it didn't matter that she was a dog and I was human. We shared something deeply ingrained within. No matter what, I was going to save her too.

In the meantime, however, I would care for her rescued son. Her precious puppy. I would use what I'd learned to give him the best puppyhood and life possible. I know now that what I felt then was plain old compassion but that it would take root and blossom the way it did, change my life so completely, couldn't, at that point, have been further from my thoughts. I was just following an instinct and would follow it without question to do the right thing.

The place where I'd been instructed to meet the transport was a big, sprawling stables in the middle of open countryside. It was part of the pet transport business that was bringing my new puppy to me and who were considered the best by the many people I spoke to in the dog rescue world. It was one of several such businesses that operated between the UK and Romania, transporting the rescue dogs coming to the UK for rehoming. They were also one of the legitimate ones, unlike many others, which often caused confrontation and conflict between the different rescue dog transporters.

Already I had learned a fair bit about the business of adopting dogs in Romania. Since the fall of Ceaușescu's communist regime in 1989, a huge stray dog problem had been building all over the country: with so many people moving to apartments where they were not allowed to keep pets, abandoned dogs, left to roam the streets, had been breeding unchecked. And with their numbers growing fast (almost none were spayed or neutered, despite various initiatives), the situation had escalated out of control. Such public shelters as existed were increasingly struggling to cope, with so many animals being rounded up by teams of state-paid official dog catchers. And, with money to care for them, or humanely euthanise them, being pocketed by corrupt officials, they were treated as vermin, subjected to unbelievable acts of cruelty, many often poisoned instead of being put to sleep and sometimes brutally killed. There was a good reason such places were known as 'kill' shelters.

The level of cruelty was staggering, and also increasing, but, because of the internet, it didn't go unnoticed. It wasn't long before the problem of Romania's street dogs caught the attention of social media and groups concerned with their welfare began mushrooming up everywhere, such as Friends of Animals in Need, pioneered by the late Judith Stuart. Also, it wasn't long before appeals (requests for help, requests for money for food and neutering, requests for medicines, requests for homes) could be seen all over social media. And, perhaps inevitably, another kind of new and profitable business took root – those who facilitated the mass transportation of dogs to the UK for rehoming, where so many people, seeing their plight, wanted to adopt them.

More and more were adopting dogs and puppies, and many did not know enough to do so correctly. To keep a dog in a home, you need to understand what a dog needs, and for a dog that has been traumatised, or lacks any social education, the odds are stacked against them staying in those new homes, the expectations of their new owners simply too high for the dogs to have any hope of fulfilling them.

I didn't want my dog to become one of those statistics so I'd done a great deal of research. I'd learned everything I could from the leading people in the dog world and was determined that if I was going to take on this puppy, I was going to do so properly.

This was a new experience for me. To consider the consequence of my actions before putting them in place had always been alien. I was making informed choices and learning to do things differently. It would turn out to be the first of many insights and life lessons I was going to learn from him.

And now here I was, having pulled into a horse yard in Essex, shaking with nerves as I climbed out of my car, and breathing in air heavy with the scent of fresh horse manure. The smell was intense, but it was one that didn't faze me. I'd grown up in the countryside and it was a smell I associated only with good things. All my life I'd struggled with people, but animals, never, and it brought back happy memories of Caspar, the pony I had loved in childhood – he'd been given to me to ride by a local couple who owned three-day-event horses in return for help with mucking out and grooming.

I had also done lots of research into the pet transporting business. I knew there were both good guys and (very) bad guys and these people, I'd been assured, were the best; the van had air conditioning and roomy crates, and, unlike some, they made sure they had water and food. They also had that tracking app, so that anxious adoptive parents could, if they wished, follow their pets' journey every step of the way.

Which, of course, I had. And now, at last, he was here.

At least I assumed so, because not long after I'd parked, the huge transporter van trundled into the yard. It had been home for three days now to some forty rescued dogs, all of whom had been vaccinated, microchipped, had their health checked and been granted pet passports, so they were legally allowed into the UK.

With so many dogs to be collected, quite a few people would presumably be arriving, though as I had arrived early, there were so far only two others, neither of whom (nothing personal) I wanted to engage with, so I kept myself a little apart and avoided making eye contact. I'm good at masking my emotions, as I have decades of experience doing it, but all I really wanted was to go in like a one-woman SWAT team, get my puppy and return to the sanctuary of home before anyone could wander over and try and talk to me.

The back of the van was being opened now and faced with two options – to risk having to mingle, or to take some sort of action – I opted to head straight to the back of the van while the others waited by their cars to be called. I went up to the young man who was pulling down the steps and asked if I could go in and meet my puppy.

'Er, I don't see why not,' he said, even though there were probably plenty of reasons why not. But my 'don't ask, don't get' routine had apparently served me well. Since he couldn't think of a reason right then, he waved me forward.

Cautiously, I climbed the steps and was taken aback to find stacked rows of crates of different sizes, containing dogs of all colours, breeds and ages. There was whimpering and yapping, multiple pairs of anxious eyes looking out at me, and the over-whelming scent of dogs and urine – enough to test even the weakest sense of smell. After three days of travel, it was overpowering.

And there he was, in the last of the big crates down at floor level, a heap of fur, bigger than I'd expected, like a shaggy grey rug, dark amber eyes looking directly into mine. Eyes that reached right into my soul. Eyes that searched my face and seemed to say *I know you*.

And, in some ways, he did, because, while Celia had been fostering him at her home in Romania, I'd insisted on being in touch with her daily, via both WhatsApp messages and phone calls. And not just to check in with her about his progress, important though that was. I had wanted to get to know him and, perhaps more importantly, had very much wanted him to get to know *me*. As with a baby in the womb, I was convinced familiarity with my voice would make a difference; aid that transition and help him settle. I felt sure that hearing my voice every day would help him not to be afraid when we first met, so I'd talk to him, sing songs to him (badly), tell him stories.

And thankfully he didn't seem to be afraid. He looked tired, yes – all the dogs did – and a little lost and bewildered, but definitely inquisitive. As I approached, rather than shrink from me, he shuffled up closer to the front of his crate; by the time I got to him, his nose was pressed right up against the metal mesh. *What's happening?* he seemed to be asking me. *What's going on? Where am I?* So I did what seemed to be the right thing in the circumstances. The *only* thing. I got down on the floor and lay sideways in front of him, my head right up to the crate, so that he could get to know my smell and so that my cheek and hair were touching his fur. His *grey* fur. For better or for worse Celia had chosen for me a bloody grey puppy. Grey, my least favourite colour. Grey, a total *non*-colour. (When your mind works like mine does such things have great significance. But as of that point in time, I must embrace grey.)

I felt my panic ebb away, like a wave across shingle.

'Hello, my little darling,' I said, looking into that intense amber gaze. 'Hello, Kratu. I'm your mummy; you're home now.'

A few formalities later, I was officially the mum of a sixteen-week-old puppy of indeterminate mixed Shepherd breed, a ball of shaggy grey fluff who had crossed half a continent to get to me. A brave adventurer whose name would be Baron Kratu von Bearbum.

Details matter to me, names especially. And this was one I'd spent a great deal of time and thought choosing. Baron, because I'm the granddaughter of a Prussian baroness, so I decided he should probably have some sort of title, and Bearbum because his tail was just a little stump, and made his back end look exactly like a bear's bottom. And as the stars have always been important in my personal belief system, it seemed fitting to name him after one of those too, so I went in search of something special and found Kratu.

Kratu (pronounced 'kray-too', which is Sanskrit and means

strength) is the name of one of the seven Hindu rishis. It's also one of the stars in the constellation known as the Big Dipper, or Great Bear. Kratu also means wisdom, empowerment and inspiration – three things I've been in pursuit of my entire life, give or take. I didn't know it then – I just loved that it suited him so well – but he really couldn't have been called anything else.

A Stark Realisation

Kratu wasn't just joining me, he was joining my canine family. Which consisted of Maia, the wolf dog I'd brought with me from London, and Paqo, another Romanian rescue puppy, whom I'd adopted the previous August. Both were at the door to greet me, as always. To remind me that I was safe now. That I was home. Today, though, with sixteen kilos of puppy in my arms, it was less effusive welcome than inquisition. I'd let myself in and, of course, they'd come rushing out to meet him. What have you got? Where've you been? What's this smorgasbord of smells? Maia was so keen to see where the scents were all coming from that she jumped up into the Land Rover and immediately fell out again. And trying to get through the door with him while being cross-examined by two forceful canine noses was a job and a half in itself.

It was another job to get the pair of them out into the garden, but having done so, I could at least start to try and collect myself and begin to process the enormity of the decision I'd made and the reality of what I'd taken on. This puppy was my responsibility now. No more directing Celia on how to do everything. This was my living, breathing, quite-a-deal-larger-than-expected, soft-furred pup. They say be careful what you wish for. This was that very moment: I had exactly what I had wished for. My little-big Kratu, another dog. Another mouth to feed. And the puppy in my arms was already a *lot* of puppy – perhaps destined to be the biggest dog I'd ever owned. As I held him, I could feel his heart beating against my chest. As of now, I was going to be his world.

I stumbled around – when overloaded by emotional stress, I can trip over my own feet – and felt suddenly overwhelmed. All I could think of was that his life was in my hands. Had I done the right thing? Had I taken the right steps? I had done my research, I had overseen his care and socialisation, I had put Celia – poor tired Celia – through all sorts to get here. I must call her, I realised, though we rarely chatted on the phone. (She was very shy about speaking English. She is hard of hearing in one ear, and also worries about her accent.) I must send her a photo to let her know our joint mission had been accomplished; of Kratu safely delivered into my arms. I drew him a little closer to me then, to breathe in that lovely puppy smell, and then got a huge whiff of stink. Travel stink. Which meant bath time should be imminent. (Puppy smell is heavenly, travel stink less so.) So, I wouldn't call her just yet. Right now, I had a puppy to settle in and all the time in the world now to question my sanity. Which, me being me, wasn't difficult.

For all that I struggled with human relationships, I have always had a connection with animals so it was no surprise that it had been another dog, Hero, who had set me on the road I was now travelling. It was Valentine's Day, 2013, when I saw him looking out at me from a rescue page on Facebook. And when you've spent as much of your life in a state of sadness and distress as I have, you develop a sixth sense for spotting it in the eyes of others. As soon as I saw his, it was like a punch to the solar plexus. I knew instantly that he needed me to help him. And help him, I decided in that instant, I would.

Being impulsive in that way was a fundamental part of who I used to be. And for much of my adolescence and early adulthood it had got me into serious trouble. The sort of trouble that invariably led to more and greater troubles: trying multiple drugs, leaving home at just sixteen, trusting strangers and being hurt and even injured as a consequence, taking risks, becoming addicted to Class A drugs, including heroin, and, during the darkest times, even attempting suicide. I never thought about consequences before doing anything, always acting on my immediate impulse. And, having jumped in when others would sensibly hold back, I could never do anything by halves. By the time I was in my mid-thirties and fully immersed in that world, I was Charlie Big Potato in everything I did. And though I didn't know why, I was also emotionally naïve, because I had no idea how other people's minds functioned.

Or what made *me* function, and it had proved to be a dangerous combination, each step along the road having taken me closer to a life in which I had to make harder and harder choices. I was soon immersed, and trying to survive, in a world of drugs and crime, a modern underworld, which is every bit as dangerous as it is painted. Many times I'd survived being beaten and had been kidnapped and raped. I ended up making it work for me on my terms, but it cost me dearly; my life subsequently, looking back, was like a kind of living death and the only way I could function was by absenting myself totally, replacing relationships with people – something I increasingly recoiled from – with the cold but less terrifying embrace of chemicals. Had I not made the choice to walk away when I did, I don't for a moment doubt that it would have killed me.

The first wake-up call that I needed to make changes was a diagnosis of hepatitis C in 2011, almost certainly due to sharing notes when sniffing cocaine. The second was the breakdown of my relationship with my then teenage daughter, Scarlett, to the extent that I realised that my responsibility as a mother meant getting her away from my chaotic life in London. Away from the excesses and a crazy, sometimes dangerous lifestyle that I was determined she was not to be part of. Away from the constant conflict between us.

I had sent her away to school to try and give her some stability, but this in itself created more problems. Communication between us, always difficult, was increasingly painful and I realised that only if I took *myself* out of the equation were things likely to improve. Sending my daughter to live with her father's family in Hertfordshire when she was fifteen was one of the hardest things I had ever had to do.

But if Scarlett was ever to become an independent, happy woman I needed to stop fighting with her and let her live her life, and go away to try to find out who I was, and why. So I went in search of spirituality and different healing methods.

Looking into healing ways, I found this was something that came naturally to me. I could do these things and realised I always had. I was hungry for knowledge so I did a lot of workshops and the diplomas began pouring in.

I had a foot in two worlds now: the healing world and the underground world.

For a while I found it easy to be in both but then I began to realise my views and values were changing. As I understood more about pain, trauma and energy, and how they resulted in loss of personal power, I started to work on myself and my perceptions started to alter, which meant my view of people and the world started to change.

I found people paid a lot of money to learn something which I found easy and although I encountered some jealousy, I continued to learn; this was something that I was good at and brought me joy. Going into shamanic trances was easy too. It was another thing I realised I had always done in times of great distress; by being hurt I had somehow found the ability to leave my body and go to another place. It was an ability that I now had no doubt had saved my fragile mind.

But I was also in conflict with what I was doing and how I lived.

I continued to change. And with that change came to the desire to learn more. Rather than designer clothes, I now began to fill my home with crystals, stones and feathers.

One workshop I attended was with a Peruvian teacher Don Amérco Yábar – he spoke my language; the traditional ways and beliefs of the indigenous Q'ero people, and after buying and reading a book about them by Joan Parisi Wilcox, the mountain Ausangate, home to Machu Picchu, called to me. It felt as if there was a long fibre of light attached to me, pulling me up into the sky and over to the mountain.

That became my reality. I made it happen. I got on a plane and flew to Peru.

My life was about to change again.

Peru was a magical place, but also a place full of lost souls. And despite great healing and deep mystical spirituality, there was also a lot of darkness. Some of the best cocaine comes from that part of the world so as well as spiritual education there were always lots of parties and, for a time, I still enjoyed living a hedonistic life alongside the spiritual.

It was there, surrounded by jungle, where I'd come to a stark realisation.

Ayahuasca is a sacred vine containing a psychoactive compound, DMT, which, cooked down into a viscous liquid form, is drunk by the indigenous people as a medicine for all types of ailments. It's also become popular with Westerners looking for enlightenment and answers to the meaning of life. To an extent, as a consequence, it's been exploited and its true meaning as a medicine has been lost.

I wasn't looking for enlightenment, but a cure for my hepatitis C. I was in Iquitos when I took it, in a jungle *malocca* – a hut where they perform ceremonies – and Percy Garcia, a respected practitioner, was the ayahuasquero, or plant ceremony facilitator. ('Shaman' is incorrect here, being a Siberian word.)

Everyone had drunk their little cup of 'the mother', as the medicine is locally known. Then we waited, around four of us, sitting around the edges of the *malocca*, for whatever personal multicoloured visions, and teaching, were to come.

At first nothing appeared and I felt remarkably lucid and wondered if I'd see anything at all. And so I was more than a little surprised when in stepped a giant Jessica Rabbit, followed by these tiny gangsters with machine guns. She sashayed across the floor of the *malocca* and they followed her, sinister as only cartoons can be. I still felt lucid; disconcertingly, everything felt normal apart from Jessica Rabbit and her retinue of gangsters, who were circling her, muttering incomprehensibly. I'd heard that other people had these amazing visions of magical beings and beautiful, phosphorescent, multicoloured backgrounds – the jungle, the animals, the plants, the starry sky – so how come I got cartoons?

Then as quickly as they'd appeared, the characters disappeared. In fact, everything had gone and the *malocca* had come back into focus. A very clear voice said, 'Why are you drinking me? You know what to do. Go and do it.'

That was the end for me. I did know what to do. I'd been given clear direction from an ancient sacred source, which I trusted. I had to go home. I would never find myself galivanting around the world.

The only place to go to try and find yourself is inwards.

No turning back now.

I left Peru shortly afterwards.

CHAPTER 3

Not Bloody Grey!

Despite the education and insights found in Peru, on my return
to the UK, my relationship with my daughter still distant and
difficult, I felt as lost among my own species as I always had. Also,
I still had hep C. But here, my obsessive need to research – to find
out, to know – led me to discover that there was a groundbreaking
new clinical trial for hepatitis being trialled by St Mary's Hospital
in Paddington. I was only the second person in the world to have it.
Or, rather, *do* it, because it involved injecting myself in the stomach
with interferon – a naturally occurring protein used to treat many
diseases of the immune system – and a protease inhibitor, on a
weekly basis for the best part of eighteen long months. By this time
I had my dog Maia and without her by my side, I'm not sure I'd
have been able to see it through.

After my injections, I would lie in bed shivering with pain and
she would lie with her back against mine. In the Andes they called
that back-to-back energy exchange. It was how the Q'ero people
– often heavily laden and, at such high altitude, with little breath

available – would greet one another if they met while on the road. They would align their backs and perform this simple but powerful practice: *may all the good energy in me be exchanged with all the good energy in you*. It was almost as if Maia knew this on a higher level – it comforted me a lot.

So, it had been gruelling, but it had cured me, at least physically. And for perhaps the first time in my adult life, I felt I'd achieved something important, having packed away the partying and in my commitment to get well, battled on through something so arduous. That in itself had given me resolve: to shut the door firmly on all the horrors of my past, which, in turn, gave me space to look forward to a potentially brighter future. Everyday emotions, I know, but for me, revelatory.

But, despite this new hope, I still had the heaviest and saddest heart. It felt like I had a block of ice in my chest, so immobilised was I by pain and guilt. So perhaps it was my soul that was calling out for meaning and in those canine eyes, I found a possible answer.

Hero was one of two dogs in desperate need of a home, having been rescued with another dog, Pola. He was injured (it was later confirmed that he'd been shot) but had loyally protected Pola from attacks by other dogs. I nicknamed him The General. He was so very loyal and upright and noble.

I still have no idea why Hero affected me the way he did. I just had this powerful sense that he needed me and I knew I could help him and Pola. I couldn't adopt them myself – they needed to stay together and Maia would never have accepted another adult female in the house – so, on impulse, I called my friend Sophi in London and begged her to take both of them on.

Sophi was a dog trainer and the friend who had given me Maia. And more importantly, she had shown me great kindness, and was always there for me during many of my darker moments, with a glass of wine, a smile and no judgement. She also taught me about dog behaviour and their diets; as well as being my friend she was my mentor.

After my experiences in Peru I had learned to embrace my wild side; my being, as the Q'ero people say, '*salka*', which means wild, undomesticated energy. I also loved wolves (also *salka*) and knowing that, she helped me find Maia. Then, to my astonishment, she gave her to me as a gift. Such kindness without expectation was something very new for me and it touched my heart deeply.

I asked Sophi if she'd foster Hero and Pola, with a view to finding homes for them. To my delight, she said she'd adopt them herself. And, though I didn't know it then, my own future was decided as well. Within weeks I had immersed myself in research into rescue, I had read everything I could find about the plight of Romania's dogs and though I knew it would be a challenge (these dogs often have serious psychological problems, much more of which later), I wanted to find another dog for myself and a suitable companion for Maia.

By now Sophi, who'd become as passionate about rescuing dogs as I was, had become a patron of the charity Friends of Animals in Need, which was how I came to find Paqo. Again, it was pure instinct that made me sure he was the perfect dog. Those eyes again – black, expressive, set in a chocolate brown face – and with markings that made him look like a monkey. But it was his kind temperament and easy-going nature that stood out most for me. He'd been discovered in a forest just outside Timisoara in western Romania, his cries so like a baby's that someone went to investigate, to find a puppy whimpering and crying, dragging itself along on its front legs, his rear ones unable to bear his weight. He'd been born with bad hips, probably from a malnourished mother. This was the stark reality of malnourished dogs having puppies. Had he not been found, he would almost certainly have perished.

This was also my first introduction into dog rescue corruption and how some so-called rescuers actually took the donation money meant for the dogs. I had one row with Paqo's rescuer and nearly lost him as a consequence: I had paid her for good-quality food and saw he was being given the cheapest and in response to my anger, she nearly stopped him coming to me. I had to eat humble pie and it tasted very bad, but I'll eat it with custard and cream if I have to.

I took Paqo home in August 2013, by which time, having been fostered, he was in much better health, though I was still careful, never allowing him to go up and down stairs or jump off things. Even in healthy puppies this can damage growing joints.

At that time, I was recovering from double bunion surgery and would be hobbling around in my 'recovery shoes', hideous blue things that I called my 'Jimmy Poos'. Going to bed every night involved me balancing Paqo on my lap, then bum-shuffling us both up the stairs as I couldn't get up them any other way and he definitely wasn't allowed to.

Paqo, incidentally, didn't come to me as Paqo – he was 'Paco'. But since the Q'ero name for healer is '*paqo*', it felt appropriate. While in Peru I'd been initiated as a *paco* in a ceremony known as a *hatun karpay*. So, the new name felt right. But just *how* right I was to find out a couple of nights later when I was woken in the small hours by a blinding blue light followed by an enormous clap of thunder. Half-asleep and terrified, I immediately yanked the covers over my head – always the best solution to make scary things go away. But I immediately thought of Maia and Paqo in the adjacent bedroom. I had few fears for my wolf dog, Maia; already I'd told her she was going to be nanny and in charge of bedtimes. But what about Paqo? I listened hard. Nothing. Not a peep. Not a whimper. Reassured, and with no further thunder or lightning, the big fearless Peruvian explorer stayed firmly hidden under the safety of the covers and eventually drifted back off to sleep.

The next morning, I went downstairs to find the phone socket on the hall carpet was now a heap of charred and twisted plastic. It had melted and blown clean off the wall. In the Andes, the tradition is that if you are a true *paqo*, you have the power to be struck by lightning and live to tell the tale. I would take my near miss as a thumbs up to that.

Nanny Maia did an incredible job with Paqo. His indoor manners were amazing, his personality delightful. And only once did I ever hear him let rip. Which took the form of a wolf wail – a full-on, full-blown howl. No guesses who he learned *that* from.

So, they had bonded, which was good. Paqo clearly loved Maia and in return, Maia nurtured him, albeit in her aloof, wolfy way. But it soon became obvious that I was very much the third wheel and although I doted on them both, I recognised they were more orientated to their own group. Yes, I was part of it too and their pal, but I felt very much on the outside looking in. So, much as I loved them, there was still something missing: a dog whose greatest bond would be with *me*.

I set about finding Kratu with the same dedication that I applied to all my chosen tasks and the attention to detail that characterised everything I did. I'd given Celia a specific and important list of what to look for. I wanted a large breed puppy, one who'd accept Maia and her nature, a GIANT (I'd used the caps lock to emphasise the point when I'd messaged her), but one who had the softest, gentlest heart.

These details were important. Maia played hard, because that's what wolfy girls did. Her power and strength, and her intensity, were a fundamental part of her. She'd get a gleam in her eye sometimes and play a little *too* hard, pushing the boundaries just enough that things could get a little wild. Not a problem for Paqo; he was her shadow, her best buddy. He had emerged as her almost-equal – a fearless pal, who had let loose his Count Pacula, slightly demonic side. I used to marvel at their antics, teeth baring, paws slapping, mouths grabbing, as they rolled around. Like two hairy WWF wrestlers, but with teeth.

But outside of their relationship, I knew any new dog Maia was going to live with needed to be a dog who could withstand her wild ways and not feel inclined to retaliate. A lot to ask, but over the time I'd known Celia, we'd learned a lot from one another. Me from her, about the harsh reality of life for Romanian dogs. And her from me, about dog psychology, behaviour and force-free reward-based training and – something sadly still so rare in her country – ways of training and socialising puppies very early with consistency and kindness, so they have the best chance of leading happy adult lives.

It wasn't always straightforward, as this was all very new to Celia, and I constantly had to check and re-check how much she had taken on board. (One of my more extreme character traits was/is repetition. She did get a lot of reminders!) Armed with that knowledge, I knew she understood the kind of puppy I was looking for.

Weeks passed and then finally, just after Christmas 2013, Celia got wind of a Roma camp just outside Cluj-Napoca in Transylvania, where she thought they might have the large breed types I wanted so much. She'd been contacted by a lady who worked for a local NGO, who'd been trying to persuade them to get their dogs spayed and neutered. She'd had no luck, but there were puppies there and she knew Celia was looking and alerted her to go and see for herself.

Having never visited the Roma camp before, Celia was apprehensive about going – such places have a reputation for good reason. But she eventually plucked up the courage, taking with her a friend called Ana Maria, who loved photography and would document everything they found. On arrival, after being allowed into the compound, a dirty, scruffy, young boy, holding up a dirty, scruffy puppy, approached them. A frightened pup.

She's since told me she knew immediately he was The One.

It might seem fanciful to some, but I had the strongest sense, even then, that Kratu was directing operations, because this was not the way it was supposed to be. I'd done all my research – piles of lists, meticulous planning, no stone unturned. My Prussian bloodline (Prussian generals were famed for their planning) was at last finding expression within me. I had also found that I was a natural with divination methods and multiple ones spoke to me: tarot cards, pendulum, Toltec omen reading, crystal ball. At times, I would use these ancient ways to confirm that my belief, and my direction, was the right one.

So, I'd expected that Celia would get in touch when she got there and leave the choosing of a *specific* puppy to me because that had been the plan. It was therefore quite a shock that, having sent pictures of poor, wretched Beauty, she sent another – of the scruffy, dirty boy holding up the scruffy, dirty puppy. The *grey* puppy. It seemed Celia had gone off track – instead of following my instructions, like me, she'd followed her instincts and chosen him.

The colour grey bothered me. I didn't know why then, but colours matter to me greatly. Not just grey, but beige too, and pastel colours generally. I was drawn to the bright, the bold, the different – these resonated greatly. I had nothing against *any* puppy, obviously. Grey, though ... And, in any case, how could Celia be so sure?

But it seemed Kratu had chosen me. How else to explain it?

'I've found your puppy, Tess,' she told me. 'I just *know* he's the one.' She didn't know why, she admitted. He just *was*. His face, his eyes, his energy ... She just felt she *knew* him. No discussion. He was mine and that, apparently, was that.

One of the things that I liked about Celia was that she wasn't afraid to stand up to me and we had some humdinger arguments as a result. This wasn't one of those times, however. If a little miffed, I respected her decision.

So, she took him that day. She couldn't not – she was too fearful about what might happen to him. All the dogs and puppies were starving, filthy and frightened, and she knew she had to get him out of there. Out of danger. And get him to me. That was no small job in itself. He'd need to see the vet, be wormed, have a basic health check and the first of his vaccinations, and highest on the agenda, since he stank to high heaven, was a bath.

All of this she did. Part one of my master plan accomplished. I have so much to thank Celia for.

My Prussian grandmother, who lived in Germany, was called Baroness Emma von der Goltz. My mother's mother, she was, for all her many virtues, imperious, stern and remote. When I was young, we would visit her at her home in the spa town of Bad Oeynhausen, where children were very much tolerated rather than welcomed; I was once banished from the dining table just for getting the giggles when I found a hair lurking in a bowl of cherries.

Looking back, I now recognise that my grandmother was from another age, one where children were expected to be seen and not heard, and any childlike behaviour was frowned upon, however natural or joyful. Maia, for all her virtues, is my grandmother's canine equivalent. Once her initial inquisitiveness about the new arrival was satisfied, she took no further interest in him, preferring to amuse herself outside and summoning her Count Pacula side-kick. Bring the puppy back for inspection only when he is civilised, she seemed to say. Though in Maia's case, it's due to trauma as well as genetic tendency. She was bitten in the throat by another dog at just twelve weeks old, which is the sort of thing that tends to shape your world-view. In any case, every dog has their own personality, character and temperament. Indeed, perhaps Maia and I were psychological soulmates. Her wolf ancestry (particularly Saarloos – a breed known for its stand-offishness and initially bred by crossing an Alsatian with a European wolf) was almost certainly key to her aloofness, just as mine was inherited from my maternal Prussian forebears. We were also both free spirits, slightly aloof, and just preferred to keep humans at arm's length. So, where others might find her distant, I accepted and embraced it. And for all her foibles she was loyal and, my goodness, she'd stood by me over the years.

Unlike Maia, my little teenage tearaway Paqo (still only nine months old himself) was keen to engage with his new playmate. But as Kratu was exhausted, the play was going to happen another day. First, he needed to settle after such a long, tiring and scary journey, and have the travel aroma gently washed from his fur. So, I bathed him and dried him (neither of which he objected to), then took him, on a lead, for a couple of walks around the garden before feeding him (both his own food and a little of the lamb I'd cooked for my own dinner) and bedding him down for the day in the new crate I'd prepared for him. Again, this was familiar; Celia and I had crate-trained him together over the phone, in preparation for the long journey here, where he'd be confined in one. On my instruction, Celia introduced him to a crate, leaving the door open, with a soft bed and a toy inside. He soon learned that this was a warm, safe place, and it soon became his preference to sleep in there. This was key to him managing his confinement coming over to the UK, which I wanted to be as stress-free as possible.

Crates are a useful training tool for puppies, keeping them out of danger and mischief, like chewing wires and furniture, and counter-surfing. They must not be used as a punishment and, when the dog is adolescent, they should be allowed the freedom of the house. Some adult dogs still like to use them, and leaving the door open to allow their choice is essential. They know it's a safe space and are relaxed inside. If your dog faces a medical procedure and they need crate rest, crate training means you are well prepared to manage this.

With everything done, I had some food before utter exhaustion kicked in and then collapsed in an armchair with a glass of wine. It had been a long, stressful and momentous day. I didn't know just how radically my life was about to change, though. Not at that point. All I knew was that every time I looked into Kratu's eyes, I was experiencing something I had never known before. Something so intense that it made everything else fade away. I was diving, that was it, and not just into his soulful infinity-pool gaze. This was something new. Something different. Something I had never felt before. Emotions were so hard for me, so fraught and complex, and the moments I knew I had encountered love had been rare. As I held him in my arms, it was as if we were no longer two separate souls – we had merged. My old life had died and this was the new life – in that moment, I couldn't tell where my arms stopped or his paws started. We were becoming one: *ouroboros*, the never-ending circle – was this my opportunity to go round and start again? Was this a new beginning for both of us?

The hardest journey we ever have to make is from the head to the heart. This can take a lifetime and a lot of self-awareness. But with Kratu, in that precise moment, I could feel something happen. Something unexpected. I felt a peace I'd never felt before. It was that easy to recognise; it was the beginning of love. I hadn't just come home with a puppy, it was more powerful than that. For the first time in my life I had arrived in my heart. And in my heart, Kratu was waiting.

We were home.

CHAPTER 4

Down the Rabbit Hole

I had always been a solitary child. Not so much lonely as separate. Disconnected and lost in a world I couldn't understand or navigate, I lived mostly in my own world, avoiding people, preferring to talk to trees, flowers and animals – things I felt I *could* understand. I had a dialogue with the natural world – it was as if nature knew me. I didn't know why. I didn't ask why. I was just aware of this gift (though at the time I didn't see it as such) of being able to understand trees and stones and animals, and other energies that people not like me didn't seem to see. A special kind of ability I suppose I didn't really think about as a child and that would take me decades to find a name for.

If I couldn't be outside – my preferred place – I would curl up and read. And would gladly have disappeared into the worlds of the books I dived into. I wanted to be in Neverland. I wanted to ride Black Beauty. I wanted to go down the rabbit hole. I wanted to step through the looking-glass. Drink that potion, eat that little cake and converse with animals in a magical world. More than anything, I wanted to be transported to Narnia, where the trees, plants and animals would all talk back to me. By far my biggest wish, though, had been to meet Aslan the lion when I got there, because I loved him with a childish intensity.

Now I looked down at Kratu, overwhelmed with that same intensity of emotion. It was getting late and I knew I should head up to bed. But must I leave him? I wasn't sure I could. Not if I hoped to get a single wink of sleep.

I never sleep well anyway. While my childhood was made difficult by my struggles to connect with people, it was made infinitely harder by the abuse I suffered at the hands of others. Even into my adult life I experienced mistreatment by people I trusted. I don't want to dwell too much on those people who caused me such pain, but these things have shaped not only my early adult life but who I am today. They have left another legacy too in the form of lifelong bulimia.

Also, it is because of them that when Kratu arrived, I still struggled with post-traumatic stress disorder (PTSD), which means nightmares and night terrors still hit me hard, courtesy of unwanted visitors when I was younger that had tried to take advantage of me. Often, I just rest with one eye open. I can still to this day wake at the drop of a pin in abject fear, thinking someone is in the bed, trying to get hold of me, and am immobilised with terror for some minutes while my brain frantically tries to grasp the reality that there is actually no one there but me.

Having decided now, I made up a bed so we could all sleep downstairs. I was beginning to feel sleepy as Kratu circled around, finding his comfy spot and then settling in among his soft blankets and toys with a contented little sigh. And as I watched him, I thought, how on earth did this precious moment come into being? How had this come to happen to *me* after the life I had lived?

Tired as I was, now that I'd asked the question, my mind's eye and memories insisted on answering – and in full HD, on the personal cinema screen inside my head. It flickered on. The Old Story Channel, one I was all too familiar with, as I'd watched so many repeats, on so many sleepless nights, and for so many decades. Who I'd been and was now, the life lessons I'd had to learn and the many horrors and traumas experienced along the way, the memories of which now started running through my head in far-from-glorious technicolour …

I'm in London, sixteen, racked with grief and despair, in a squat in an ex-council block of flats in Lambeth North. My dad died last year and now my boyfriend's gone too. Dead from an overdose. I cannot process any bit of it. All I know is that I must say goodbye to him. I walk blindly towards the place where I've been told he is 'resting'. I pass a florist. I need a flower but I don't have any money.

I go into the shop, barely able to speak, tears cascading down my face.

'Please can I have a flower? Just one? My boyfriend is dead and I want to say goodbye with a flower, but I haven't got any money to pay for it.'

Visibly moved, the shop owner hands me a red rose. 'Don't worry about the money,' he says. 'This is a gift, take it.'

I thank him but inside I am full up with pain and anger. Fuck the love from people. They only leave you …

I'm in the flat I share with Tony, in Brixton Hill. I don't know what I've done to provoke it but he's coming towards me with half a pool cue in his hand, his eyes squinted tight as the red mists descend. He lifts his arm and lays into me, repeatedly striking my

legs with no let-up and no mercy, despite my screams. I know his mum is upstairs but she doesn't come to save me. I tell him to fuck off, shout it over and over, but the more I do so, the more and the harder he hits me. He only stops, I realise, when he knows he is likely to put me in hospital and I finally make it out of the front door, sobbing, battered and barely able to walk.

I'm squatting in Islington and I'm on the street, walking. I have a needle and syringe containing heroin hidden within the pages of a book. I'm on my way to Sian's because, having tried and failed, I need help to inject it. I knock on her door, ask for guidance.

'Come in,' she says. 'I can help.'

It's late evening and I'm in the club where I'm working as a topless hostess, having given up the stripping as I hated having to dance. Numb to the core, I get money to buy the heroin I now live for by earning commission persuading punters to buy expensive but cheap-shit champagne. Tonight, as with most nights, I seize every opportunity. When the punter looks away, I pour half a bottle of the fizz onto the already sticky floor. It never fails. He thinks he's finished it and orders another ...

I'm at the GP, finding out I'm expecting a baby. I have been using for six years now and am already six months pregnant. The horrifying reality hits home in an instant. If I don't stop – right now – my baby will be born addicted too. A powerful and instinctive force seems to come out of nowhere. I demand that the GP admit me to hospital, both to check the baby's health and so I can get clean.

Fortunately, he's kind and, by now, knows me well. Within a week, I'm an inpatient at Queen Charlotte's Hospital, in Hammersmith, where I remain till my child is born and we are both clean.

It was as painful as ever to watch all those movies. Realising what I'd lost over the years was my personal power, each person who hurt me taking away a piece of my heart and soul. I had worked hard to get through all I had. Even, at times, just to stay alive. And so, after a childhood and adolescence of hardship, an early adult life of excess culminating in my trip to Peru, I had finally earned my peace and, consequently, I had also earned Kratu. I owned that right now. It was mine. *He* was mine.

I had been judged harshly all my life for being 'too much'. In all I did, in the way I was – it was always 'too much'. The biggest critic of all had been me, though. I had lived with self-hatred and self-blame for most of my life now, so that a little puppy could look at me with love and accept all of me, without judgement, was the most liberating feeling I had ever experienced.

On that note, the personal cinema screen abruptly turned off. The ever-open eye flickered a few times before gently closing and I slept.

CHAPTER 5

A Multitude of Masks

I greeted the dawn full of curiosity and excitement about the newest member of my little clan. And the strangest thing happened. In the weak morning light spilling through the window my scruffy grey puppy looked partly golden. He was the most unusual colour I had ever seen.

Just seeing that suffused my heart with light. It all seemed to fit. He didn't look grey at all now – yes, there was *some* grey, but he was unquestionably mostly golden. My Golden Child. My Sunshine Boy. My Chosen One. In short, he really was, I thought, my very own Aslan. Bizarrely, as well as the distinct golden stripes, he also seemed to have grown feathers; here and there, throughout his coat, I noticed there were long plumes of black, which looked more like they belonged on an ostrich than a dog. When did *that* happen? I'd never seen anything quite like it.

I certainly hadn't seen it the previous day. It was evident that in my state of exhaustion, I hadn't had time to inspect him closely. Now I ran my hands over his beautiful, soft, gleaming puppy fur with these frond-like black floaty feathers. He was like a magical beast. I was amazed. He loved the contact and wriggled closer, and I could feel his puppy warmth as I buried my nose into his now-clean fur. There is something about the smell of puppies and babies, something delicious.

Looking at Kratu now, it hit me hard that he was real. I was struggling with my emotions about finally having him here, with me, but also from the sheer enormity of what I realised I'd achieved. I wasn't used to achieving things – to wanting things and actually getting them. And now I had actually manifested what I'd wanted, the reality of my responsibility to Kratu scared me. It was almost as if I was holding a bubble in my hands. A thing of such beauty and fragility. The slightest slip and it – *he* – could disappear before my eyes. Was he *really* mine? I had too little self-worth and self-belief to accept that I was good enough to have such a precious thing as this.

Kratu was, in short, the embodiment of everything I had ever had on the wish list I had given Celia. Maia, with her aloofness, and Paqo, with his wackiness, were already happy with each other. The whole point of seeking Kratu was for me to have such a connection for myself; somebody I could communicate with on the deepest level and who wanted to communicate with me. I wanted and needed a best friend too.

Kratu, meanwhile, was busy just being a puppy. As soon as I let him out of the crate he was anxious to explore again – a brand new day and new adventures beckoned! I could feel the energy of his excitement flowing through him. First things first, though. On the lead, and straight into the garden, to do what he had to do. Letting the dogs out was the first item on my daily routine, obviously. And today I would go with them to direct operations, so I pulled on my dressing gown and trainers and followed them into the garden. It was another beautiful sunny day, the dew catching the dappled rays and twinkling like small stars all around the garden. The air was warm, the birds were singing and there was the happiest puppy ever, gambolling around, sticking his bum up in the air and being such a clown. It was a very special moment in time.

I'm a great believer in toilet training for puppies. Name it, then, as soon as they do it, reward it. Wee wee. Watch and wait. Then 'Good boy!' Then a treat. Poo poo. Watch and wait. Then 'Good boy!' Then a treat. As with so many things with dogs, the repetition and consistency are everything. Some learn fast, others more slowly, but in the end, they usually do learn. You just have to keep repeating what you want and rewarding them when they do it. So I followed Kratu around the garden till the mission had been accomplished and you could almost feel the pride coming off him as I praised him. He knew what to do and he was proud to be able to show me, then he was off again, as if the very grass made him want to jump for joy.

He was a kind of cross between a spring lamb and a particularly mad March hare, with this curious joy in sticking his bum right up in the air, which he seemed to do at every opportunity. My very own little Aslan had arrived and was keen to explore his kingdom. To discover, to experience, to unearth that joy. Because what was life, he seemed to be trying to tell me, as he monkey-climbed all over me, if not one big amazing, joyous adventure? I don't think I'd ever seen so much delight and happiness concentrated in one place at one time and his evident delight at being with me touched my heart.

Finally, someone who wanted to interact with me!

Maia and Paqo didn't know quite what to make of this explosion of fluff and feathers, but even on that first day I could sense Kratu was working some kind of happiness magic. He must have because

I wrote on my Facebook post that day that Maia must have been abducted by aliens. Yes, she looked the same, smelled the same, but she was just being so *nice*. Had another dog been put there in her place?

Over the next couple of days, as our little family began to bond, I became aware that the glimpses of lightness I'd started feeling came accompanied by something else too. We'd be in the garden and I'd catch my reflection in a window, and I'd realise that it wasn't only Maia who'd undergone a change: I was seeing myself smiling.

It was impossible not to smile. Kratu's antics were just so funny. But I never smiled. Smiling was not something I was used to doing. I didn't get most people's humour; I didn't get jokes. I found so many of my interactions with other people so stressful that a mask of cool indifference was my natural way of being because an unemotional demeanour felt easier and safer. Yet here I was, with my dogs, with this clown-puppy holding court, giving my face such a workout that the muscles in my cheeks hurt. Once or twice I even caught myself laughing.

But through all this joy a sobering thought came to me. Kratu's joyful freedom and ability to express himself was so far removed from life for many dogs in Romania. Some are left to run feral, never knowing any home other than the streets. Others are chained up all day and night, denied even the smallest of freedoms. The freedom to play, to run about, to feel any pleasure in simply existing. Working dogs only ever worked, the majority just had to endure.

Had I ever felt pleasure in simply existing? Yes, way back, when outside in nature or with my pony. But when that, and my childhood, were both taken away from me, life had become little more than a painful daily battle to survive. But that child was still in there. Was that her? What was this song I could hear, vibrating from deep inside me? Could it be a child singing? In happy days, so long ago now, I used to sing to my pony, as we trotted along tracks and country lanes, always deeply embarrassed if we encountered an unseen human. Then the healing songs sung during plant medicine ceremonies, called *icaros*. It was a song, it was little Tess and she was singing her lilting happy song.

In this new and strange, happy, in-the-moment feeling of joy, it was as if someone I hadn't been in contact with for a very long time had woken up from a very deep sleep. I'd kept little Tess, as I thought of her, safe for my entire adult life. It was only by protecting her out of sight in the shadows that I'd been able to function during the worst times and survive. Looking at Kratu, though, the little girl in the dark was peeking out. It felt safe for her. She'd woken up, she was aware.

And she was curious.

By now there was no question I knew quite a lot about Romanian rescue, but being faced with sixteen – no, now *seventeen* – kilograms of this particular Romanian rescue puppy was a different matter. He was a whirlwind, a now-stripy Tigger, his hairy bearbum in the air, and doing roly-polys just for the sheer pleasure of it. Which was joyous to witness. He wasn't so much a glass-half-full puppy as a brimming-over puppy. His exuberance, his essential Kratuness, simply could not be contained. And he was growing – so fast I could see it happening before my eyes. But he still had a lot of growing to do.

So, time was of the essence and if my master plan was to stay on track, his introduction to socialising in the UK beckoned. Time to take him out and introduce him to Ely. We couldn't hide away at home forever.

The natural world wasn't a problem. There were plenty of wild places in the Cambridgeshire Fens where we could walk and be sure of not bumping into anyone. The bigger part of my programme, however, was to start socialising Kratu around people and to continue the work we had started with Celia, learning that touch was a kind and gentle thing, so that visits to vets, groomers, etc. and meeting people would be stress-free and something they'd be comfortable with. It sounds self-evident. And for most people, I imagine, it is. When faced with a beautiful and charismatic puppy looking up at them, the natural urge for most people is to say, 'Oh, he's gorgeous! Can I stroke him?', and doing so is positive for both human and dog. It's also important to foster that trust in a puppy from the outset as there will be times when human touch is necessary for their welfare. A dog who has never made that positive connection will be anxious and frightened and in some extreme cases fear can quickly turn into aggression. In short, I had wanted to teach Kratu about all the kindness in the world, the polar opposite of what I'd experienced.

I had made that head start with Celia while she was fostering Kratu in Romania. At that time, she knew nothing about kind, reward-based dog training – it simply wasn't a part of Romanian culture. So, I'd sent her daily tasks and, in keeping with our agreement, she reciprocated by sending back videos of her completing them with Kratu, of her touching him and stroking him; gentle little touches, on his head and ears, along his back, his legs and paws. Picking them up and examining them, looking in his ears … All very gentle, lots of 'good boys' and lots of rewards. All great groundwork for those first necessary vet visits. Plus, it was always in my mind that every day Kratu experienced kindness as a young puppy was a day that was going to contribute to his adult world-view.

This mattered greatly to me, even more than it had with Maia and Paqo. Maia, being a wolf dog, had a different, unique energy and made it quite apparent that anything more than basic training simply wasn't happening as it was of zero interest to her. Additionally, she was a home girl, not really interested in a social life anyway.

Paqo, on the other hand, had done really well with his puppy classes and had had some rally training as well as basic obedience. He walked to heel beautifully, he was a delight around others and I was more than happy with his progress. However, it was clear that his and Maia's main bond was with one another – they were happy as they were and I was happy with that. Also, they both had a switch-off button for going any further, so there was no point – it had to be enjoyable for them too.

Kratu was different: he was going to be my partner in crime. I had believed it and now I felt it – our connection was to develop to the point where it would eventually become unbreakable. I also knew there was more to life than could be found in the sanctuary and safety of my back garden. Yes, I was scared, but that was also my 'normal' and certainly did not stop me living life. I still had a thirst for excitement and adventure and there was an element of me that liked living on the edge.

I was now going to quench it with him by my side.

And now Kratu was with me, the work to achieve that must continue, ironically despite my own experiences of human touch, particularly during the worst times in my life, having impacted on my own perception so negatively. The Toltec belief is that how you see life is bound up in the experiences you live through: you learn to see through your own filter system and I filtered everything at that time through my experiences of feeling fear, doubt, mistrust, pain, sadness, brutality and trauma. But that wasn't *all*. I at least had a memory of love. The precious memory of the love I'd felt for Caspar, my pony, when I was eleven, and the love I'd received from him in return. This had been the distant shining light in my darkest times. The little burning ember inside me. That alone was the tiny spark that had saved my life. I had once known love. It would go on to be buried beneath a huge pile of shit, but it was still there.

My perception was starting to change. Already my life had been changing, putting Maia and Paqo's needs before my own, but with Kratu, whose needs were far more specialised, the change was now really accelerating. Being determined to make his life happy was key to a lot of those changes. Yes, it would be hard being around people, but I would just have to tough it out. I had my repertoire of masks and I could find one to wear that suited the inevitable occasion when someone would ask me if they could stroke him. I would smile and say, 'Of *course* you can,' when I knew every part of me would be cringing from the contact and my ADHD (attention deficit hyperactivity disorder) would have me twitching and twiddling, my eyes glazing over, ants in my pants and desperate to be gone.

And by far the most important thing was that I did all of this with sincere intent. It would be hard, but masking, copying confidence, appearing outgoing, relaxed and calm were all things I'd learned to do over decades (they had even saved my life on a few occasions). They had stood me in good stead before and now I needed to dust these qualities off again.

It especially mattered that I could hide the gut-churning fear from Kratu. Dogs are incredibly attuned to our human body language and if he felt my anxiety, he would pick up on it – the opposite of what I wanted to achieve.

Which was where my intent came in. Using intention is a powerful tool. When I stir my coffee every morning, I set my daily intention for any possible battles I might be facing by carefully choosing my weapons. These might include honesty, forgiveness, research or education (and, if none of those work, a kick up the proverbial!). My intention was now to hide my anxiety from Kratu and show him that interactions with strangers are easily done. Which, to put it bluntly, meant shoulders back, head up and getting on with it.

Time for an education for both of us.

CHAPTER 6

Prussian General Genes

After a few trips into Ely to test both mine and Kratu's mettle, our first big outing was to the Offord Dog Show and Fun Day, in August 2014.

I wasn't sure about the 'fun' part, but at least my confidence was growing. By now I was taking Kratu on a weekly basis to a lovely trainer called Mel Thomason and, at seven months, he was coming on in leaps and bounds. (Though, in reality, *not* by doing leaping and bounding, but instead some really lovely heel work, with the odd leap and bound thrown in for good measure.)

Although I was nervous, I was at least no stranger to those kinds of shows. Though my childhood was blighted in so many ways, I had memories that still shone a bright and happy light, among them going to country shows with Caspar, my pony. What I mostly remember was the euphoria of winning rosettes; for those brief interludes in what was mostly such a sad and lost childhood, it would make me feel I'd achieved something, that I mattered.

There was no doubt that I would have to battle with my fear and anxiety to do this, but then I always had to do this because that was my normality. And having set my intention to do it, it was a challenge I was determined to take on. The event was also local, so I knew that there was a reasonable chance that I'd have the reassurance of seeing a few familiar faces.

Even so, I left home that morning not just weighed down by drinks, snacks and treats for Kratu, but by the ridiculously large knot of anxiety in my stomach. I had no expectations other than to get there, survive the day and get home feeling I'd done something good for my boy. It was also a great way to see how far we really had come with our training. Would he walk to heel? Resist the urge to jump up? Would he listen to me with all those distractions around him? This was going to be an opportunity to find out.

But then something happened to me. I don't know why, but as soon as we had parked up and walked into the showground itself, a sudden crazy impulse took over. Before I could talk myself out of such folly, I went straight over to the registration table, paid the entry fee and entered Kratu in the Best Puppy category.

The fallout from my decision soon came hurrying along to join us. My heart was beginning to pound, nervousness was kicking in big time and as I looked around me, I felt overwhelmed. So many people and animals, so many big noisy families, their children running around, licking ice creams, waving balloons around, shouting and laughing. So many colours. So much going on. The assault on my senses felt immense. I felt the noise as a tangible force inside my head, bouncing around, kicking my skull, hobnail boots on.

I began seriously regretting what I'd done now. What was I thinking? I would have to take Kratu into the ring now, along with all the other puppies, which meant along with their owners as well.

I spoke sternly to myself again. That was exactly what we

were here for. For challenges and obstacles to be met head-on and overcome. Otherwise fear won the day and I was not having that – I had already fought too many battles to get this far. So, I summoned the Prussian general genes: time to walk tall and carry on. Head held high, shoulders back. 'Come on, Kratu,' I told him. 'Let's do this.'

But he didn't need telling – he was absorbing everything around him with pure joy. He was in his personal nirvana. People! And scents! And new friends! And *more* scents! Dog bottoms everywhere – delicious! But while his muzzle was in the air, sniffing the nose candy around him, I really didn't know what I was doing. So, I stood and watched a couple of the other classes so I understood the logistics, which seemed to involve joining the other competitors and standing in a row, with the judge moving along it, a bit like the Queen does after a Royal Variety Performance. Then, after every dog had been properly inspected, everyone had to run up and down in a line, so the judge could observe the dogs in motion.

All very straightforward, at least in theory. And at least helped by the fact that the judge looked so friendly and approachable. She was young too; not at all the sort of person you'd visualise if anyone said the word 'judge' to you. Even so, when the time came for the Best Puppy class, my anxiety, ever-present, was intense. I was also concerned about doing it wrong and people laughing, or Kratu launching at the judge and me falling over, and us both making spectacles of ourselves.

I needn't have worried. When the judge reached us, to my relief, all four paws stayed on the ground, but there was no mistaking the warmth of Kratu's greeting. He was so delighted to make the acquaintance of this lovely new person it was as if they'd been best friends forever.

The judge looked equally smitten and, still basking warmly in her evident adoration, Kratu stepped up a gear when it came to the next part. As I started to run, he began moving alongside me. And with such poise! His paws lifted up and off the ground almost as if he was floating on air, the canine equivalent of Rudolf Nureyev.

I lack the grace of Margot Fonteyn at the best of times and was now also hampered by having brought a bag with me that was the size of a hamper, which bumped annoyingly alongside us, containing, as it did, everything bar the metaphorical kitchen sink.

Another lesson learned, I thought, as I bounced, bump-bump-bump, alongside him. Whose idea was it a) to have brought the bag in the first place and b) not to put the thing down before I ran? Then another thought bumped along – brakes! Oh my goodness, would we stop in time not to go flying through the rope barrier? I couldn't see my feet – damn you, bag! – so was I going to trip over them? I was being swept along now, as if propelled not just by a ballet dancer but an elemental force, and with all that kind of stuff busy flying through my head, I only just managed to do the required 180-degree turn to avoid zooming straight through the barrier. Then back again and flowing to a halt in front of the judge and just about managing not to knock her out with my bag. Forget Kratu, it was *me* who was the one with a lot to learn, or so it seemed. Showing dogs was an art I badly needed to perfect.

That bit done, it was now a question of lining up again and waiting while the judge placed the puppies from last to first. There were eight entrants and each time her lips parted, I braced myself. Surely eighth? Okay, seventh, then. Sixth? No, it couldn't be. Fifth? *Surely* fourth? – I was trying to second-guess her mouth now – and if not, then – not third … And not second! 'And the winner,' came the words finally, 'is Baron Kratu von Bearbum!'

It was the first time I'd heard his full name on another person's lips. It was Kratu. *My* Kratu. We'd done it! My mouth fell open in sheer disbelief. We had to walk into the middle of the ring to receive our rosette and as the judge shook my already shaky hand and made a big fuss of Kratu (who was basking in his glory), it felt so surreal it was as if I was dreaming. But then came the news that we needed to be present a while longer: winning the Best Puppy class meant that Kratu was automatically entered for the Best in Show.

I left the ring in total amazement and with an hour or so to kill was pleased to bump into some people from the K9 project in Ely, a canine café I'd visited with Kratu and Paqo a few times, and who were running a stall there.

There were some very beautiful dogs in the ring, so I was beyond shocked when, once again, Kratu's name was called out as the winner of Best in Show, and after that everything was a bit of a blur. So many people came up to congratulate us – including the mother of Dee, the judge, an equally lovely lady who would go on to have a soft spot for Kratu until her sad passing in 2020.

Needless to say, for Kratu the day had been exhausting, but what a wonderful education too, as it had given him the taste of an audience enjoying his performance. It was also the day when for me it hit home that my shaggy grey-golden dog was turning into my polar opposite. He liked people. He *loved* people. He wanted to be around them. He thrived on the sort of contact I flinched from. So the winning was about more than a rosette and trophy, it was about me doing, and being, something good.

That early belief that I *wasn't* good was so deeply ingrained in me that I carried the memory of our achievement at the Offord Dog Show around with me for days. I decided that we were going to do more. Kratu was a very handsome dog and pulled out all the stops with his outstanding movement. He loved performing in the ring and he excelled at it too. Where I had such a lot to learn, he was clearly a natural. He stood out from the crowd and that was enough for me to start to check on Facebook for more dog shows.

More than that though, it was confirmation of something that would go on to influence almost everything I did. There was something about this dog of mine that made him like a hairy magnet. I'd seen it so often and this really proved it. The way people were drawn to him, the way that, despite his size, no one ever shied away from him, the fact that everyone wanted to talk to him and stroke him, and how everyone he met seemed so mesmerised in his presence.

Yes, he clearly loved it – he actually seemed to glow – but it wasn't just about that. He had a gift: he made people smile, and he gave them happiness. They lit up around him. Most dogs dislike eye contact because they find it intimidating, but Kratu could catch a gaze and hold it in a way I'd never seen before.

The Q'ero people had already had a very profound effect on me. Their simplicity, their sense of community, their love for the mountains and stars, their energy-clearing and healing methods and their sending of *despachos* – prayers and sacred offerings of thanks to Mother Earth. These things already resonated in every atom of my being. And the more I learned from them, the more I had applied it to my life.

One major tool that helped bring change for me was learning about *hucha* and *sami* energies. One is heavy and the other light. If you are full of the heavy *hucha* energy, your life is hard work, negative emotions are present and even illness, depression and sadness. *Hucha* energy is created in life every day. Being stuck in a traffic jam, stubbing your toe on the door, being lied to, hurtful comments, being cheated on, shouting and anger. Fear is a big cause of it too. These are all heavy energies which we encounter daily. Some of them stick around. Some of the heavy sticky energy blocks are from the past; trauma and bad experiences we have hidden because we are unable to deal with them. This all stops us moving forward in life and becoming who we are meant to be.

Then we have *sami*, which is light energy, and is created by acknowledging the blessings we often take for granted. The sound of birdsong, the look of love when I gaze into Kratu's eyes, the sound of a child's laughter, the blue sky, the scent of a flower; those beautiful, joyful and uplifting observations and moments create pure *sami* energy, as do the kindnesses and help we offer one another.

There are various techniques to clear *hucha*, engaging with *sami* energy being one of the most powerful ways. Willingness to engage with change and learning tools to make change happen, clear the past and anything heavy or that doesn't serve you well is also a wonderful place to start. Nothing happens unless you work at it. There is no instant solution or enlightenment. No magic potions will make anything happen either. Only you, yourself, can actually do it. You don't have to share my beliefs or have an interest in Q'ero ways to apply these principles to life, but learning about these ideas and daily energy practices impacted me hugely and helped me on my own path to healing.

I was now learning to clear the old heavy *hucha* energy and replacing it with light *sami* energy, and Kratu – named after a star – was the embodiment of that shining, flowing energy. It was a new beginning, a rebirth, and one I was so ready for, having let go enough of my past to be able to receive it and be grateful.

There is an Andean belief and way of being called *Anyi*, which means 'to reciprocate'. It's a core Q'ero concept, and the main rule they all live by, since they believe everything in the world is connected. I had been given a gift, a very special one, and I intended to share it: I would train Kratu to become a therapy dog, so others could benefit too.

In the meantime, I had other plans afoot. As Kratu was blossoming with his training, my education in Romanian dog breeds was stepping up a gear too. By now I'd been involved in the rescue and rehoming of Romanian strays for getting on for two years. They came in all shapes and sizes, had a wide range of personalities and, tragically, not all had had the outcomes we'd hoped for, as they were all too often placed in inappropriate home situations, leading to escapes, returns to rescue centres and, tragically, dogs sometimes being put to sleep. And having Kratu in my life could only heighten my sense that the rescue business was less than perfect. Many people were well-meaning with their placement of dogs, but they weren't understanding enough of what those dogs needed to stay within a home.

So I researched, scouring websites, joining groups and speaking to different breeders, picking the brains of anyone I could find who seemed to know what they were talking about and discarding the many chocolate teapots in those worlds along the way. And the more I researched – something I loved, something so ingrained in my personality – the more I learned.

My research bore fruit. Based on what I'd learned from the Roma (that Kratu's father was a large Shepherd dog) and from the photographs of Beauty, I knew Kratu was Carpathian and Mioritic (*miora* means 'sheep'). Both were breeds used as guardians in rural Romania to protect flocks from predators such as wolves and bears. In other words, powerful animals, bred for strength and independence, and for scaring off creatures that were bigger than they were. Dogs of enormous courage and resilience, and independent thinkers, as they needed to be to make decisions when guarding their flocks.

My obsessional nature kicked in more and more as I researched. There was no doubt that Kratu was already the luckiest puppy. To the best of my knowledge, he was the only pup ever to have left Romania armed with the sort of education and socialisation that would enable him to fit into UK life and to have a positive outlook. That was just not how things normally worked. Even leaving aside the opportunists who bred and traded puppies just for money, the best-intentioned rescue outfits struggled to give the dogs decent care, many spending weeks in overcrowded shelters, fighting for space, food and attention, and left to their own devices with no human intervention for long periods of time.

Which was why it mattered. The first few weeks and months are so important to a dog's development and world-view and though a minority of shelters interacted with and handled their dogs, it was in a very basic sense – they just did not have the skills to teach them. The majority did not handle their dogs at all. And not just from cruelty, but a lack of caring and empathy. What to show puppies, what to teach them – many simply did not have this knowledge and were not interested in gaining it. They were motivated only by the ever-increasing adoption fees, which could range from £300 to £500. I've since heard of one woman asking as much as £800. And though social media gave the impression that kind contact with the dogs was becoming more widespread, the reality was that when the camera was off, any positive contact with the dogs was off too. Left to their own devices, in a large group setting dogs could bully and fight one another and engage in behaviours inconducive to going on to have happy lives as family pets.

Puppies learn from other dogs, so if their experiences are harsh, then it's no surprise that they soon learn to be the same. They don't have access to any training, walking on a lead, or of the noises from a world they need to survive in once homed, until one day a dog bus comes along, they have a long, traumatic journey, at the end of which, exhausted and traumatised, they are unloaded into a stranger's arms and taken straight into a family home. That is why so many of these adoptions don't work, or the dogs run away or react with fear, possibly leading to aggression. And it's understandable. After all, what do they know of washing machines, vacuum cleaners, televisions, cars and traffic? For the street dogs who've only ever known open spaces, to be suddenly confined within four walls must be terrifying – no wonder they would often try to escape.

Rescue puppies and dogs also need time to decompress. As dog behaviourist Andrew Hale tries to get people to understand, 'There must be NO busy walks. NO inviting loads round to meet the dog. NO expectations on how a dog should be. Twenty per cent of dogs get returned in the first two months, many because the owners have not given the dog time to decompress and find their way.' I found that number so sad. And frustrating too, as, with patience and education, so much is avoidable.

It was becoming clear too that, much as I had learned, I still needed to know more. If Kratu was going to go on to have the best life I could give him, then I needed to see these dogs, native to Romania, *in* Romania, to fully understand specific breed information and to see for myself how they were and how they lived. And there was only one way to do that: to travel to Romania myself.

But that wasn't the only reason. Since Kratu had come to me I had never stopped thinking about Beauty, the mother who'd given birth to him back in the depths of the freezing Transylvanian winter. The pictures Celia had sent of her had broken my heart. Now that Kratu had settled in and I felt comfortable leaving him, there was another reason for me to make that trip to Romania: I'd made Beauty a promise. And I intended to keep it.

CHAPTER 7

In the Land of
Wolves and Bears

I set off for Luton Airport just after dawn on a warm day in late
August 2014, leaving the dogs in the care of a trusted friend,
Casey, who'd moved in for the week in exchange for a bit of
pocket money to put towards her fund for university.

Casey was sixteen and a neighbour. She lived with her parents
a few doors down and once again, it felt as if Kratu had chosen
her. I'd been walking down the lane with him and Maia not long
after he'd arrived and he'd been most insistent that the young girl
gardening a few houses along the road was someone we needed
to get to know. So, we went over and he greeted her as if being
reunited with a long-lost and particularly cherished friend. I took
his lead – his very presence was giving me the confidence to chat
to her – and she had such a good energy about her. She also loved
dogs and was eager to learn, and began coming out on walks
with us regularly.

Friends sometimes come into our lives when we need them but

least expect them. There might have been years separating us but with Casey, I felt an instant connection. We were both solitary, a bit boho, and felt that same connectedness to nature. Her dream was to eventually run an animal sanctuary and I don't doubt for a minute that she will. I knew the dogs would be safe and happy in her care.

Cluj-Napoca International Airport couldn't have been more of a stark contrast. Having negotiated Luton, then endured a flight next to a man who coughed and spluttered the entire way, the arrivals hall was a vision from hell. So many people, such bright lights, too much going on all around me, and hard surfaces everywhere on which sounds bounced and echoed and were flung in all directions. I felt, as I always do when my senses are overloaded, as if I was being crushed – like Alice in Wonderland, I was getting smaller and smaller. The urge to run away was almost overwhelming and I really identified with the urgent need to flee from confinement that those street dogs must have felt. But to where?

Celia was supposed to be meeting me but there was no sign of her anywhere. And once my phone came alive again, having found a new place to connect, a flurry of texts confirmed that she'd left scant time to get there and park, and having been unable to do the latter – she was still circling the car park – wouldn't be there for a while yet. However, knowing her arrival was imminent meant I could calm down a little and also check in with Casey to make sure the dogs were okay, so by the time we met, which was the first time we'd seen one another in the flesh, I could at least breathe. I was here. Stage one complete. I needed to smile at her; she was making a huge effort for me. Mask on, anxiety hidden, I felt ready.

Celia was in her late thirties, shorter than I'd realised and with a kind, slightly nervous smile. I could feel the warmth spilling out of her as she apologised for keeping me waiting. Immediately I knew that she had a good soul. Though we'd only just met in person, she already felt like a friend. We still had another wait, though, for my travelling companion, Carol, who was arriving on another flight, an hour later.

I hadn't originally intended to make the trip with someone else, but we'd been chatting for a while on Facebook and it turned out that Carol was keen to see the Roma camp too. She had adopted her dog, Ottie, through Celia and me; I'd fostered Ottie when she'd first come to the UK. Like me, Carol was eager to see where her dog had originally come from and she seemed like a genuinely kind and caring dog owner.

In hindsight, given how much I need my own space to escape to, I don't know what possessed me to agree that we share a hotel room. Sometimes I just make ill-informed choices. Because greeting her at the airport, and realising how chalk and cheese we appeared to be, the thought of sharing a bedroom with a virtual stranger seemed like a very bad idea indeed. But it was done and I'd just have to deal with it. If it all got too much, I would simply take myself off to the hotel bar for a glass of wine. If it *really* got too much, perhaps two.

I had never been to Romania before and my first impression as we drove into Cluj-Napoca that day was how busy it was. We were in the thick of the rush hour and it seemed no different from any other busy city. Noisy and fume-filled – a world away from my rural existence back at home. But at least there didn't seem to be any dogs on the street. I'd learned so much by now about the dog catchers, and the way animals were routinely rounded up and killed, that had I seen any cruelty, I would have struggled not to go steaming in. Instead, I could settle back in Celia's car and take in the view.

A prosperous university town, Cluj-Napoca wasn't dog-catcher territory, thankfully, and parts of it were reminiscent of Prague, with its stunning architecture and imposing clusters of venerable old buildings. But there were also pockets where the economic reality for some was all too evident: grey buildings, dirty streets, signs of poverty everywhere. A reminder that this was a country in which the post-Ceauşescu economic growth hadn't filtered through to all, even nearly thirty years later.

Celia, though initially surprised (and perhaps a little anxious) that we'd wanted to visit, turned out to be a warm and enthusiastic tour guide. She took us out that night (and every subsequent night), keen to showcase her city and for us to try some of the local food delicacies, including a pale creamy soup called ciorba de burta, from which I took a single sip and didn't take to. I suggested Carol try it, and, politely, she did. And, as she liked it, she finished it, only for the reality to be revealed … Sitting at the bottom of the bowl was a pile of pale, frilly tripe worms. Which looked about as appetising as *real* worms. I don't know what came over me, but this caused me to have a terrible attack of the giggles, tears running down my face and setting Celia off too.

Carol, however, clearly didn't find it funny. Realising that, coupled with her look of utter shock at my hysterics, I reined in my mirth. I hadn't meant to cause offence, but I had a hunch that it would set a less than friendly tone for the entire trip. I really don't help myself sometimes.

The following morning, relations polite rather than cordial, I knew I was coming down with something as I woke up with a pounding, fuzzy head. My principal feeling was one of irritation and annoyance. I had so much to see and do and could do without *this*. Still, at least it set a tone that would go on to prove useful as I was definitely in no mood to be messed with.

Celia came to pick us up and drive us out to the Roma camp – a job she'd told me more than once she didn't relish. So much so that at first she said she couldn't remember the way. But I was having none of it and eventually, she conceded. 'But some of these people are very dangerous people,' she warned as soon as we climbed into her car. 'And very suspicious of anyone poking about. Some drink,' she added darkly. 'They might become violent.'

Bring it on, I thought. And I meant it. I'd survived plenty of encounters with drunk violent men. Plus, it was the morning.

As soon as we left the city it was as if we were going back in time. The outskirts quickly gave way to scruffy scrub and farmland and though the wooded hills and mountains rose impressively in the distance, the land here was agricultural, open fields, with herds of sheep grazing in the distance, though the pasture looked thin, sparse and coarse.

The country people lived in tiny ramshackle houses, dressed simply, and some were still travelling by horse-drawn cart. And running everywhere, among the detritus of human occupation, were dogs and geese and chickens. This was the countryside of myth and fable, I reminded myself. Home not just to people but, in the more remote parts of Transylvania, also wolves and bears.

Once we arrived at the camp, which was a few hundred yards from a small military base, Celia told us to wait in the car while she checked that they were amenable to being visited. Apparently, they were, as one of the two teenage boys who'd come out looking over at the car and nodding. Celia beckoned us over.

I'd seen pictures, of course, but they couldn't prepare me for the reality. As I climbed out of the car, I looked around in disbelief. Such buildings as existed were crude and in a bad state of repair and the scattered outbuildings we could see were made of random planks, sheets of cast iron and pallets. Weeds grew in and up everything, and the place was liberally strewn with what looked like building rubble and piles and piles of rubbish.

There was a big dog chained up, who looked over at us despondently, and other smaller dogs milling around, noses close to the ground, presumably in search of anything to eat. I thought of Kratu and the sort of life he might have had if he'd stayed here. No playing, no happiness, no gambolling around carefree. He would have been starving, beaten and chained, and the thought shocked me. What were the odds of him being chosen for his new life with me? Non-existent.

I approached the boys with Carol, who seemed happy not to engage and just observe. The bigger of the two looked cocky and suspicious of us, holding himself with that veneer of swagger that teenage boys do everywhere you go. But they were curious. They asked what we wanted (Celia translated for us as they talked) and she told them I had adopted one of the puppies from Christmas and had wanted to see where he came from. Upon which, the smaller of the boys turned and walked over into one of the outbuildings, then reappeared dragging a filthy and terrified bitch behind him, her teats hanging down so far they were close to dragging on the ground, her eyes full of hopelessness and fear and pain. The penny dropped.

They said something to Celia and she replied. I heard the word Tutty.

It was her. The one from the photos that I had called Beauty. Kratu's mother. She had another litter already; this was Romanian puppy farming in action. Every season a litter with no break from it, ever. I had never seen teats like hers before, never seen such heartbreaking despair.

'Is that her?' I asked Celia.

She nodded. 'Yes, he says she is called Tutty.'

She had a name: it was Tutty and she was their prize breeding machine.

The poor wretched girl.

'She has had more pups,' the boy told Celia in Romanian. 'You can take two of them if you want?'

Celia translated, while my woozy head tried to take it all in. She'd had another litter and two were marked for trading with a Shepherd. The other two were of no use to them, just more mouths to feed. The boy said we could take them if we wanted to. They were, basically, surplus to requirements.

I told Celia to tell him we'd take the two puppies they didn't want, whom the other boy had now gone to fetch. I noticed he'd gone to get them from a pile of old pallets – where their mother kept them for safety and shelter. All the time the dog I'd first seen looked on from the distance. Another Shepherd, thin and mangy, who had what looked like a nasty wound on his head. Who was he? Another of Tutty's offspring?

Celia went up to him and stroked him. He seemed such a good-natured dog that it made things so much sadder. Meanwhile, the older boy still stood holding Tutty in front of us. He had his hands around her neck, forcing her head upwards, and the whites of her eyes told me everything I needed to know about her distrust and fear at being close to them.

I wanted to drop to my knees. Wanted to stroke her. Wanted to tell her that everything would be okay. That I was going to take her away from this place. But I knew I mustn't. I didn't want to distress her any further. And neither did I want the boys to see how much I cared. I couldn't let them know. If they thought she was something of value to me, they might feel more inclined to keep her. She was a cash cow for them in any case – supplier of puppies. Though, in her emaciated state, how many more pregnancies could she endure?

So I stepped back, not forward, and put on a mask of indifference; the hardest mask to put on in that moment. I could talk from my heart though, so that's exactly what I did. Spoke directly from my heart to hers. *Tutty, I'm coming to take you away. You have to know this. I heard you, I know your pain and I'm going to help you. From one mother to another, I have your son. He is safe. I love him so much. Your two little girls are safe too. Now it's your turn. I need you to stay strong, Tutty. Do not give up now – come on, girl. I need you to feel this and hear me. I heard your prayer, I came. You are leaving this godforsaken place.* The struggle to hold back the tears was immense, but essential. So I managed. For Tutty I held them back and instead willed those words into her head.

The boy brought out the puppies. Shaggy bundles of fluff and not too thin. Despite her sorry state, Tutty was keeping them nourished. I told Celia to tell the boys that we'd take the two puppies they had no use for and to ask how long before they were able to go. Celia did so. The boy told her four weeks.

That agreed, we said we'd return in the morning with food for Tutty. If they wanted us to take the puppies off their hands, there was no way we wouldn't do this. I then told Celia to tell them.

We then left, Celia increasingly nervous that if we hung around too long, the grandfather might come out and start laying into all and sundry – including us: 'We need to go,' she said, 'it's dangerous.' And I was happy to go. I knew I'd struggle to keep my indifferent face on for much longer and might open my mouth to let them know how I felt about such abuse. But I had my eye firmly on another goal now. Grandfather or not, I was going to get Tutty away from these people. If it came to it, I'd have even gone straight back into Cluj-Napoca, found some underworld connections and some muscle for hire, and paid them to come out here and take her for me. The fire that had been burning in my belly now burned even brighter.

I was going to rescue her, no matter what it took.

CHAPTER 8

Heart to Heart
with Tutty

The next morning, we went to a supermarket in Cluj-Napoca and bought sacks of dog food to take to the camp so that we would at least know Tutty was being fed while she continued to wean her puppies.

The teenage boys seemed happy to see us. There was no sign of Tutty today and I wondered if she was staying hidden. I hoped they hadn't been rough with her overnight. But they brought out all four pups for us to look at, handling them with the same harsh indifference as they had the previous day.

I wanted to shout at them to stop it, to handle them more gently, but, again, I kept my mouth shut as even the smallest hint that we might be judging them might see us run out of the camp.

Then came the business of negotiating to take Tutty with the man who was in charge – something I'd thought about at length the previous night. I knew she'd be valuable to him, having supplied litter after litter, so on the way there I'd told Celia exactly what she must say to him. She must tell him I was a stupid woman from the UK, who loved rescuing dogs, but didn't really know what I was doing. She should let him know, I went on, that I was looking at several other dogs, but that I rather liked Tutty and I *might* be persuaded to give them some money for her. She should also point out – this bit was obviously the most important – that Tutty was getting old and wouldn't be producing puppies for much longer. And I could see by the glint that had appeared in the teenager's eye as she spoke that my carefully tended seed had been sown. He would speak to his uncle in London, he promised, where he was currently away, apparently 'on business'.

An old man had emerged from one of the outbuildings now. Short and wizened, years of hard living were etched into his face. He wasn't physically imposing, but there was something about his expression that made me sure no compassion was likely to be found there.

'This is the grandfather,' Celia whispered as he approached us. Then, after some incomprehensible rapid dialogue between him and Celia, he grabbed a puppy from the smaller boy and threw it down onto the ground. He then made a scissoring motion over its tail and muttered something to Celia, and I realised he was telling her he'd cut off their tails for us.

'Nu!' she said, waving her hand at him. 'Nu! No cut! Do not cut!'

I felt sick to my stomach. Had this happened to Kratu? Celia had told me she thought they did it so that when the dogs got into fights there was no tail for them to get between their teeth. It was also traditional because of ancient beliefs – it was thought that when a dog was curled up asleep, with its tail over its nose, it would hamper its ability to smell danger. A third reason was pragmatic: if a dog didn't have a big bushy tail, it meant less time spent getting thorns and burrs out of its coat.

I thought of Kratu's nub of tail, his bearbum, such an integral part of who he was now. I had no idea what he had experienced in his first few weeks of life, but I just hoped and prayed he hadn't suffered in pain.

We had to leave the puppies, obviously. We had no choice till they were weaned. Celia would have to come back for them then – well, assuming the man in charge would allow it. More rapid-fire words in Romanian ensued. It would first be necessary for the uncle to grant his permission, because Tutty was apparently his favourite dog. Which made me wonder how his least favourite dog must be treated. But I kept quiet, my face a blank mask while Celia and the boy exchanged mobile phone numbers. They would phone the uncle, the boy said, and let her know.

Before we left again, I named the puppies Raphael and Gabriel, after the angels, because it struck me that if I was to get them away from that place, I needed all the divine intervention I could get.

The following day, feeling no better and wilting in the heat, I packed up my things, ready to make the trip down to Vâlcea, where I was to meet Anna, a rescuer I'd had interactions with on social media, and visit her shelter. Carol, meanwhile, was already heading back to the UK. Celia and I had been out for a last meal together; I wanted to introduce her to sushi and she had taken to it like a duck to water. I also taught her how to use chopsticks, which she really enjoyed. It was nice to have some downtime, just the two of us, after the intensity of the day.

Vâlcea was a vast region some four hours south of Cluj-Napoca, way too far to expect Celia to drive me. But once again she stepped up, offering to take me halfway, so we arranged a pickup point where Anna would meet me.

The first half of the journey passed quickly and pleasantly; I loved travelling in other countries and was taking in the scenery, while telling Celia about my plans for rescuing Tutty. Though I was still feeling rough from the bug picked up on the plane, so once we met up with Anna, it was good to settle back into her car – a big Mercedes four by four – and continue to let the scenery slide by while she drove. Now it really did feel as if I'd arrived in Brothers Grimm territory, winding roads weaving their way through endless dark, forbidding forests which swept across the mountainsides as far as you could see. These were the forests full of wolves and bears I had heard so much about; forests I definitely wouldn't have been comfortable wandering around in. Evocative and dense, they looked exactly like the ones I used to read about in fairy tales, the kind that would swallow up unsuspecting children, never to be seen again.

I'd met Anna on Facebook because of Mowgli, a beautiful big Shepherd dog in urgent need of a home, who was incredibly shy of people and broken down. He was another bear of a dog, and I was tempted to keep him myself, but he was older than Paqo and something in my gut told me that he and Maia wouldn't hit it off. So instead I paid for him to be neutered and followed his journey, which turned out to be an example of why these rescues so often go wrong as the woman who adopted him discarded him almost immediately – and should never have been allowed to have him in the first place as I'd already been warned by someone who knew her that she'd done this with three previous dogs. Mowgli was eventually rehomed, even more traumatised by then, by a lovely couple who had really stepped up to take him on and loved and cared for him to the end. He died of old age in 2020.

At the time Anna worked alongside three women at another shelter, but had since broken away after being unhappy with the way they were doing things. I agreed, and together we rescued another dog, Tara, and her puppy, both of whom I found adoptive families for in the UK. I'd also shared Anna's campaign to raise funds for her own shelter and managed to get her a substantial food donation so it was nice to meet her finally and see how she was getting on. Like Celia, or so I thought, she was one of the good people in the dog rescue world.

The hotel I'd booked in Râmnicu Vâlcea was a small, boutique one; this was a city that was really beginning to open up to tourists and that first evening, Anna joined me there for dinner. We had a lovely meal, for which she insisted on paying, and it was good to sit down, eat good food and have a glass of wine, and though I was struggling by the end – both for things to chat about and with my aeroplane bug – I was pleased I'd made the trip and met Anna in the flesh.

One thing we did discuss was the possibility of Tutty retiring to Anna's shelter if no home could be found for her in the UK. I'd pay for her to be spayed etc. and she could live out her life with good food in her belly and, equally importantly, in safety. It would be a back-up plan and it was reassuring to have it. I hated the thought of leaving Romania, and Tutty, without being confident that she was going to be okay.

The following morning, both the flu (as the bug seemed to have turned into) and the heat pressed down hard on my head. It was sweltering and I felt seriously unwell. I had brought a lot of donations to Romania with me, gifts and surprises for the dogs, and arrived armed with treats, squeaky toys, leads and collars. I was also really missing home and my dogs, especially Kratu, and after reading messages from the friends who'd donated these gifts for the dogs (such kind words from people who believed in me), I felt far away and very close to tears. I was determined to complete my mission though.

Anna and her husband rented a villa adjacent to their shelter, the land for which they'd been able to buy from donations. It was a compound down a muddy track, home to around a hundred rescued dogs and puppies, and on the face of it, the place looked okay. Yes, it was a bit ramshackle in places, but with fundraising help from the UK, they were busy making improvements and expanding the operation. And from what I could see, they were providing good care for the animals, cleaning out the kennels regularly, making sure all the dogs were exercised in rotation and well fed. I only saw one fight break out while I was there, which Anna stepped in immediately, and decisively, to stop, by kicking one of the dogs so hard that it flew right into the air. 'Sorry,' she said, presumably seeing my shocked expression, 'but it would have killed the other one if I hadn't done that.'

I felt uncomfortable. Should I say something? Perhaps not. And the attack *had* looked vicious. But that kick had been more vicious still.

We moved on and I tried to put it out of my mind. Ditto the hut that was brimming with donations which, apparently, were not being used. Medication, food, blankets and water bowls and so on. I was taking it all in, but I wasn't taking it *in*. Plus, I liked Anna. She seemed capable and efficient. A good person, doing her best. I genuinely thought we were on the same side.

But were we? I'd been asked by another rescuer, from the Friends of Animals in Need charity, if I could check up on a dog she'd asked Anna to pick up from a public shelter, who'd been apparently in a pretty bad way. The dog's name was Summer and when I asked Anna if I could go and take a look at her, she led me to the food and medical supply shed where they were keeping her. Anna explained that she was too weak to be put in with the other dogs.

It was another day of unrelenting midsummer heat, the temperature pushing, and perhaps exceeding, thirty degrees. To be locked up in a shed in such heat would be akin to torture and what I saw appalled me. In the suffocating heat what I saw was a skeleton on legs, huge lumps of pus stuck to the lids of both eyes, barely any fur and ticks all over her head and body.

I'm a reiki master – a Japanese technique for healing ailments and reducing stress on the body – and the woman for whom I'd sought Summer out had asked me if I'd do some energy healing on her. Energy work is based on connecting with the flow that makes physical, emotional, mental and spiritual recovery possible.

Did Summer sense that? Because somehow, she managed to get up on to her feet and totter outside with me.

I was furious. Had they any intention of helping her? I knew she had come out of the public shelter a few days previously. Had she been shut up in here the entire time? She looked up at me with eyes that were already dead; it would take little for her to give up altogether. 'No, Summer,' I told her firmly, as I led her to a quiet spot, 'it is not your time.' Then I lay my hands gently on her and with everything I could muster from my knowledge and belief systems, I prayed to the universe to save her. Every single energetic healing way I knew was channelled into this nearly dead dog.

We cleaned her eyes then and took off as many ticks as we could. No chemicals, though, as she was too weak for that. In truth, she was little more than an empty shell.

I made sure she had some food and water before I left. Sometimes prayers are heard. Not all, though. I could only hope mine would be.

That night, I was invited to the home of one of the girls who helped out at Anna's shelter, welcomed into the humble apartment she shared with her mum, who gave me a glass of delicious home-made liqueur, made from local raspberries. We then went back to my hotel and had dinner together. A very gentle, kind girl, she was studying in Bucharest and put a lot of her spare time into helping rescue dogs. She reminded me of Casey and I was really heartened to see such kindness and dedication to welfare in some of the young people I was meeting. It gave me hope that change really could happen.

I returned the next day with the pockets of my army trousers stuffed with things pilfered from the breakfast buffet: sausages, whole boiled eggs, goats' cheese. Which drove the other dogs wild as I made my way across the compound to Summer – I had to hop, skip and jump around them to get to her. And already she looked different: a light had come on in her eyes.

The next three days were a blur of activity. And almost literally: what with my woolly, woozy head and the sweat pouring into my eyes in the fearsome heat. Another rescuer I knew, from Bucharest, came to join me at Anna's shelter and between us we continued to remove ticks from Summer, using tweezers to prise them out. Her recovery was miraculous, such a rapid change. If I hadn't witnessed it myself, I would not have believed it. Soon she was strong enough to be moved in with the other dogs to sleep more comfortably in the biggest, cleanest kennel.

Anna and I had also found some puppies out on the road, teeny tiny ones, squealing pitifully for their mum. We rounded them up and took them all to the vet where they were wormed, but I didn't hold out a lot of hope for them. I also saw more evidence of the scale of the problem, as on the second day Anna told me she already had another mum and pups which she was holding currently in the back of her van.

Again, I was concerned. It was too hot to leave puppies in a vehicle. There was also a newly rescued bitch running loose outside the compound, which made no sense to me, given that she was still unneutered. Even then, when alarm bells should have been ringing, I was prepared to give Anna the benefit of the doubt. They were constantly up against it, the tide of dogs and pups relentless, and when I thought of the kill shelters (which I had opted not to visit as I knew how I would react if I saw someone inflicting pain on a dog – I would not have been able to restrain myself), I remembered that at least they were trying to do *something*. So, I bit my tongue.

I still had one job left to do. Before setting off for Romania, I'd been asked by a woman from another UK dog rescue group on Facebook if I could check on the progress of another shelter in Vâlcea, for which they had raised some €30,000 to build and support. It was an astonishing sum and testament to the kindness of strangers who really cared about the plight of these animals, so I asked Anna if she knew of it.

'Shelter?' she answered. '*What* shelter?' She pulled a look of disgust, clearly knowing something I didn't. 'Come on,' she added. 'I will take you there.'

Now alarm bells *did* ring. There was clearly something amiss. With Anna's husband driving, we made the short journey from the city and when we got there it was painfully obvious what it was. Thirty thousand euros had been sent out to Romania and all I could see when I climbed out into the unrelenting heat was a huge concrete base, grasses blowing around and through it, surrounded by a thin wire fence. The only thing inside it was a small rusty digger, standing alone in the vast empty space.

There was no one in sight. It was chilling. These people – whoever they were – had raised, and were probably *still* raising, huge sums from well-meaning strangers in the UK. From kind-hearted people, many of whom could probably ill afford to donate. And then simply pocketing it.

'I want you to expose them for the liars and thieves they are,' Anna said. 'I hope you tell people what they are really like; people must know the truth.'

At the time, still believing Anna to be one of the good guys, I took her at her word.

And it wasn't until I was back in the UK and reunited with my own dogs that I began reanalysing everything I'd seen. I wasn't the kind of person who could easily have the wool pulled over my eyes and as I began to properly process what I'd seen for myself, I realised things were horribly wrong. There had been so many things that just hadn't seemed to sit right. Celia, for instance, rescued dogs because she cared. She was an animal lover, giving her time generously, but she also had a full-time job as a computer programmer and the rescuing she did – including fostering Kratu – she had to fit in around that, often dipping into her own pocket too.

Rescuers like Anna were different: they were running their own shelters. Many were huge too – some housed as many as six or seven hundred dogs – and they seemed to be springing up all over the place and putting out appeals for help all over social media.

Romania is a poor country, especially in rural areas, yet the 'rescuers' who were asking for that help, to build and run shelters, seemed not to have any source of income. So what exactly were *they* living on while they did their good work? How did they find money to pay their own rent, let alone buy their expensive off-road cars, holidays and top-of-the-range phones?

Clearly from all those donations.

I knew I had to tell the woman who'd done the fundraising for the non-existent shelter about the reality of where the money might really have gone. I thought long and hard about it, because I didn't want to become embroiled in a scandal, but the dogs and the truth both weighed heavily on my mind, so I got in touch with her and sent photos of what I'd found.

Predictably, and rightly, she was furious. Realising how badly she'd been duped was a bitter pill to swallow and I really felt for her. But I also questioned myself. How had I not seen through what had been going on, even when it was right under my nose? Had my antennae become blunted? Could I really be that gullible? No, I thought. I wasn't. In my woozy state while in Romania, I didn't think to question where they'd got the money from. But now I was home, back in good health and firing on all cylinders, it seemed so obvious. As did the reason why so many genuinely kind and caring people got sucked in. These people were very, very good at what they did, and they knew exactly which buttons to press. I also realised why Anna had let the bitch she'd found run loose outside the compound and turn up sporadically for food: they actually *wanted* her pregnant to keep up the stream of new puppies for adoption. A pregnant bitch was a guaranteed income, because cute fluffy puppies attracted adoption fees quickly.

There was good news, at least, about Tutty. After some very tense negotiations, over a number of days, Celia messaged to tell me that the man who ran the Roma camp had agreed I could have her, along with Gabriel and Raphael, for €50.

I was on tenterhooks then while Celia drove to go and get her and on arrival, finding out she had disappeared. The old man had savagely beaten her the day before and she'd run away to save her life – she was found, terrified and shaking, beneath a bush on the edge of the property and it was only when Celia texted to say Tutty was safely in her car with the two puppies that I felt I could breathe properly again. Indeed, my heart was dancing with joy and delight: we had done it.

With Celia's help, I set about beginning the long, complicated process of organising veterinary care, medical checks, vaccinations and temporary foster homes for them all. I found a German Shepherd dog rescue who agreed to foster Gabriel (now Gabby, as she'd turned out to be a bitch) and a new home in Scotland for Tutty. It hit me hard to think what might have happened, had that home not been found. Had I not discovered what I had, I'd have let her go to Anna's.

Raffy, however, was still a cause for concern, so I decided there was no choice but to foster him myself rather than carry on worrying about him. I understood his needs. Only when I was satisfied that he could be rehomed appropriately and safely would I let him go.

But I was soon to have my eyes opened further. Once the can had been opened so many worms now slithered out that it was difficult to keep track of them all. It turned out that Anna's husband, who also transported rescue dogs to the UK, wasn't the kind man I'd originally thought him; I heard of dogs transported by him dying en route after being viciously beaten and a friend who had helped rehome two dogs from their shelter told me that when they later had them X-rayed at the vets, they found evidence of recently fractured bones.

I had finally discovered the truth about Anna. She wasn't one of the good rescuers but a very clever fraudster – happy to exploit those dogs, to steal donations. Too many little things that hadn't sat well with me all made sense now and fell into place. I also found out more about her relationship with the three women who ran the 'shelter' that had fraudulently taken that €30,000. They had all worked for the other shelter and seeing how much money could be made from them, they too had broken away and set up on their own. They were in competition, essentially, and Anna had taken me to their non-existent shelter as a means to cause trouble for the others and keep the donations coming to *her*.

In the coming months, I would go on to find many more instances of money going missing, donations of medicines, food and equipment sold on for profit and, even worse, casual cruelty on a scale I'd never seen before, with dogs left untreated for disease or injury and many dying while in these people's 'care'. It was becoming increasingly obvious that donated money wasn't going to help these poor animals, it was being channelled into the creation of ever more and ever bigger 'shelters'. This income stream then became a source of regular, easy money to spend on luxury goods, manicures, hairdressers and trips, or even to purchase land, as Anna had done.

In my dark and dangerous past I had seen and experienced a lot of dubious activities, so I wasn't naïve – I knew criminal activity when I saw it. And I wasn't surprised, either. Hardened criminals will always be with us, ready to exploit whatever opportunities come their way.

I have come across all kinds of criminals, some merciless and ruthless, others still sticklers for old school family values, some of whom I had got on well with and had had a great deal of respect for. Then there was another kind, one I disliked a lot: the kind who exploit children and animals, or the elderly and vulnerable, and are, to my mind, the very worst kind. So, I was angry about how so many kind people were being exploited. And for exactly that quality: their compassionate hearts. I was also furious that the dogs themselves were at the centre of all this and that their lives didn't matter to these people at all.

It was a dirty, corrupt industry of the very worst kind that preyed on the innocence of both defenceless animals and the naivety of caring people who were trying to help them. Abuse of the vilest kind, it was still growing.

CHAPTER 9

Teenage Tearaways

It was only a few weeks after returning from Romania that I realised that I was going to have to move home again as I was having problems with my neighbour. The thought filled me with great sadness, but I knew I didn't have a choice – my home was my sanctuary and I struggled to function if it wasn't a place of peace.

But I was sick of continually moving on. Already I had moved home seven times since leaving London, five of those while undergoing chemo for my hepatitis. Could I really face doing it an eighth time?

All I could think of, and for one of only a few times in my life, was how much I was now going to lose. I loved my house and garden, loved the neighbourhood, loved the countryside all around me and loved the few precious friends I'd made since moving there. Casey, down the lane, who would regularly join me on my daily dog walks, and Mel Thomason, the lovely dog trainer we were now working with.

My walkabouts with Kratu, so good for him, had also proved to be good for me too. It was still hard for me, but I was beginning to get better at it. I'd spent months now making those regular trips into Ely with him, to the cathedral, to the market and along the canal – basically, anywhere people thronged. And more often than not fortified by a little something from Cherry Hill Chocolates, where the owner Angie (whom I'd taken to calling 'Angie Chocolate') was, through Kratu, becoming another much-valued friend. Spending a few minutes outside her shop (she adored Kratu and loved to make a fuss of him) would help calm me for the ordeal ahead. Just as with a dog, I came to associate what I was doing with the reward of a milk chocolate truffle.

And the self-rewarding hadn't stopped there. I had an old friend called David, whom I'd known for some thirty years, and who was blue-eyed and gorgeous and played polo. So, one of the first early socialising outings my Roma camp boy ever went on was to mingle with the great and good at a polo match, of all things. And he took to it as if born to it.

In short, little by little, life was getting more balanced and functional and I was beginning to feel calmer, more settled, but one big, heavy issue was beginning to weigh me down. Sadly, it was becoming clear that staying put wasn't an option as my relationship with the woman next door was getting increasingly fractious. She had a number of cats who, like all cats, had their own ideas about territory. They would hide under my Land Rover and whenever we came out would streak away at great speed until they judged they were safe, then sit and stare, as if willing the dogs to chase them. Which, of course, they wanted to, Maia especially, and where she led, the others followed, which made holding on to them a major challenge; my aching shoulders were testament to that.

I knew there was little that could be done about feline comings and goings, but my neighbour also had five dogs, one of which was a Jack Russell Terrier who would regularly try to get into my garden. A territorial guarder, he was also highly dog-reactive, racing up and down the garden on his side of the fence, snarling and barking with a ferocious intensity. My landlord called out a dog warden, who suggested banging two tin trays together, but the only thing I felt like banging was her and my neighbour's heads together. Running around banging tin trays was both archaic (you didn't resolve anything using abusive, negative methods like this) and clearly no way to live.

The Jack Russell also, at one point, managed to break into my garden. I was able to get him out again before anything nasty could happen, but it didn't take much to realise that if there was a confrontation, my dogs, being so much bigger, would probably get the blame, despite the fact that he was the interloper. Needless to say, this made for a disharmonious relationship, though if that had been all then perhaps I could have coped, since I kept myself mostly to myself, but what really set my nerves jangling was my neighbour shouting at her dogs. I'd wake to hear her shouting. Every time I went in the garden, I could hear her shouting as well – 'Get in NOW!', 'Shut UP!' – day in, day out. I swear I could even hear her shouting in my dreams and day-to-day life was fast becoming increasingly intolerable. It felt as if we were under constant invasion.

One day it got so bad that I just lay down on the floor in sheer defeat and misery. Maia and Paqo were with me, Maia howling for her dinner before I gave up altogether, while Paqo, being Paqo, just sat down on me. (Why? Sometimes his mind truly amazes me.) I then heard a flurry of paws and peeped out to see a hairy thing approaching, his head on the floor sideways, bum up in the air. In this fashion he proceeded to shuffle his way up to me, then shoved my arm out of the way so he could wiggle underneath it, the bearbum still firmly and proudly aloft. I remember thinking at the time that I had the oddest, oddest animals, but you cannot stay down with the clowns. Determined now to change things for us all, I got up.

Because only one person in the family could change things. And that was me. So, with great reluctance, I set about looking for a house swap. Which would be no mean feat, I knew, because I knew exactly what I needed. A rural location, an open fire, a large secure garden and, ideally, open fields all around me. I didn't even care if the house was in a bad state of repair – if I could just find those four things, I knew I'd be okay. Okay, five … If at all possible, no cats nearby.

Happily, in November 2014, I found a bungalow that seemed perfect. On one side was a retired gentleman, Colin, a homebody who loved to garden, and on the other, a retired lady who was also quite reclusive. It was also only a forty-five-minute drive away from Mel, which meant I could continue with Kratu and Paqo's training classes. This was it, a place I and my dogs could call home. A place we could stay.

In the meantime, Raffy was still in Romania and I was growing increasingly anxious about him. Celia had taken him to be fostered by a friend of hers who had a farm and where the other dogs who lived there were well cared for. But this was a working farm, not a home, and their dogs spent the majority of their lives outdoors. And their job was, of course, to guard livestock, exactly what I *didn't* want Raffy to learn about.

I was also acutely aware of the trauma Raffy had already witnessed, with his mother being hurt so badly, and how much his successful adoption would depend on him being prepared for, and comfortable with, life within a family. I was trying though, regularly looking out for the right home for him on Facebook.

But that meant a stringent home check: I'd need to visit, check the garden fence and the home environment, see a vet reference, meet any other dogs and ask my long, long list of questions.

But Raffy also needed some groundwork putting in and I had my doubts that it was actually being done. It was a difficult time, because there was nowhere else for him to go and I wasn't sure Celia really understood my concerns. But she tried her best, monitoring him closely for the last remaining weeks, and in mid-November, just a week after I'd made the move from Witchford to our bungalow in Newmarket, I collected him from South Mimms service station and brought him home.

He was huge now and clearly on course to get bigger. With his bulk and his comically enormous donkey paws, I knew he was going to be even bigger than Kratu.

I kept telling myself he'd be moving on, that I *was* going to rehome him, but almost immediately it was clear that he could go nowhere until his fear and anxiety were addressed. Our lovely new neighbour, Colin, would always stop and say hello to the dogs and Kratu, Maia and Paqo all loved greeting him. Raffy, however, would take one look and growl at him, his body language nervous and uncertain. He didn't know how to manage in a new situation with new people – he couldn't have been more unlike Kratu if he'd tried.

This both worried and saddened me. I had to dig deep. Here we go, something else I don't know about and would now have to learn: the impact of trauma and what I needed to do to try and overcome it and understand his needs. He had clearly seen the living daylights beaten out of his mother with the stick and hearing her screams must have scarred him terribly.

The days seemed to melt into one another, in an endless round of caring for the dogs and thinking and trying to settle in, which was hard for me, but a great deal harder for the dogs, for whom it was obviously disorientating. There was also the important task of finding safe places to walk the dogs. One of the first things I always did when I moved was to scout around, to find the places I could walk where it was both safe for me and with no other dogs or people to worry about. Hooray, I then found it! Outside one of the huge studs was a road with the widest verge and even a parking spot halfway along outside a gate. That was it, and I could also walk more than one at a time there. I was so happy to have found it – it would make my life a lot easier.

Happily, we also made progress with Colin the neighbour. Every time we saw him, I made sure we stopped and I gave Raffy treats. Soon he learned that Colin was a kind man and not someone to be scared of. Pretty soon he would even let Colin give him treats as well, wagging his tail as he did so. Result!

It also worked both ways: I knew the dogs and I had made a big difference to his life. Colin was such a solitary soul and spent most of his time at home, tending his flowers and vegetables, of which there were many. Gardening was his life and growing his own food was second nature to him; I realised too he'd barely spent time with other people in years.

Still, life was busy and complicated. Now I had four dogs in the house, three of whom were male teenagers, fond of throwing themselves around, lots of hairy chest-puffing and general macho behaviour, and paw stamping as if they were dancing a flamenco. Another fine mess I'd got myself into ... I would often shake my head in disbelief.

I did at one point get close to finding a home for Raffy when a retiring US soldier said she'd be interested in taking him with her when she returned to the States. I'd met her in a Land Rover garage when I was getting something fixed and she seemed like a genuinely lovely person. We started corresponding by email and she was clearly keen to take on Raffy, but when she started talking about her extended family and how the dogs already in it mingled like a big extended family themselves, alarm bells couldn't help but start ringing. Suppose Raffy couldn't cope? What then? One fail-safe in my dog rescuing journey up to that point was that if things weren't working out, I could, and would, always get a dog back. If he went to the States with her, that wouldn't be an option. So I pulled out – I just didn't dare take the risk.

After that, I decided to stop looking and to accept that perhaps I'd been kidding myself all along. Sometimes I like to fool myself with a pretence even though I secretly know the outcome. And, with Raffy, I think deep down I knew I'd never find anyone who would fulfil my exacting standards. Raffy was going nowhere; my gentle giant was safe with me.

But I was now living with a bunch of testosterone-fuelled adolescents so the training continued: I was still taking Kratu, Paqo and Raffy to train with Mel every week and while there, they would all behave impeccably but carry on like hooligans at home. They played too roughly and I would be forever in and out, having to break it up before it escalated. Natural play between dogs is good, but hoodlum play is not.

I was also very aware of their lineage so I trod extremely carefully around their interactions with other dogs and kept them well away from other males, especially unneutered ones, because I didn't want those guardian genes kicking in and ruining their good natures around other dogs – something my research had led me to conclude was a real risk. So I never went anywhere where I knew there would be dogs running off the lead as too many owners lacked basic control. It didn't matter how many times they might shout out, 'It's okay, he's friendly!' Since you wouldn't allow your children to run up to strangers, then, to my mind, neither should you let your dog.

There was no getting away from it though, it was Kratu who challenged me the most. Where Paqo was definitely a biscuit short of a packet and Raffy, dear Raffy, was such a highly strung soul, Kratu's lust for life – the very thing I would go on to so cherish – was fast wearing me out. The canine equivalent of 'Don't Stop Me Now', the Queen song that summed him up so well, he reminded me so much of the irrepressible, irreplaceable Freddie Mercury.

He'd been doing so well at his classes, his good behaviour around people really blossoming, but now the teenager in him had suddenly started to kick in (as any parent with human teenagers can probably relate to) and he was fast becoming a master of mischief.

He was in the back of the car one day when I nipped into Waitrose. I'd already been to the butchers and had put a large box of bones in the front. My other dogs, having beautiful manners around food, always left them alone.

I got back into the car and did a double take. There was now an empty box on the passenger seat beside me, so I jumped out and looked in the back. And there he was, still in the process of hiding a bone, gently patting it into position with his paw. He had taken them one by one and buried them in the blankets, no doubt for later consumption. I couldn't be cross with him – he was just way too happy with all his hard work.

Worse, though, was that he had taken to launching. It was almost as if he'd grown coiled springs in his paws and, having discovered them, all he seemed to want to do was test them out, doing these enormous bounces around (not to mention *at*) all and sundry. He was exploding with verve, exuberance and curiosity, but the impulse to display what he felt at any moment suddenly accelerated. He wanted to see it, and meet it, and land on it and smell it – boing, boing, then bounce, and then ... LAUNCH!

This naturally took a further toll on my back, neck and shoulders, all of which were under great duress. So, something needed to be done, because I simply didn't have the mental and physical strength to continue as I was. Which brought me up short a second time. I had evidently failed to realise how much intense hard work was actually needed to give him the social skills he would need for his life in the UK.

It was something I took very seriously. If I don't have the skill set, experience and knowledge to achieve what I need, I will find the best people in those areas who do, so I immersed myself in research into behavioural consultants – I wanted to find someone whose speciality was behavioural training.

But I was in for another wake-up call. Because behavioural consultants, it seemed, came at a cost. It didn't take many enquiries to establish that the fees charged by professional dog behaviourists were way out of my league.

The more I emailed, the more I learned. Some people emerged as being convinced they had the answer to all problems and at £90 an hour, if they were wrong, I would pay the piper and my dogs would pay the price. Some smacked of huge ego over ability. I just couldn't seem to find the right person: someone with experience and kindness who was really invested in dogs' and their owners' welfare, as opposed to investing primarily in their bank accounts. That was what I needed to find.

Fate smiled on me one day and my search came to fruition. I found a lovely lady called Wendy Kruger at Wood Green, a charity based less than an hour from where I lived, who offered behavioural help for owners with challenging dogs, and who might otherwise not be able to keep them. Best of all was that the modest set donation they asked for was within my means.

But I was one of many and such services were in high demand. We had a phone consultation but I knew I was going to have to be patient. At that point, Maia took matters into her own hands. Around this time I was regularly taking the dogs to a doggy day care centre outside Ely, where I was able to rent time in a secure field. This was obviously heaven as they could all run together safely in a number of the enclosed play areas. On this day, however, not long after we'd arrived, another dog – a very small dog, Maia's least favourite kind – had managed to undo a door and escape from an adjacent area, heading pell-mell to the field we were in. I knew the dog and the fact that she could squeeze through the bars. As soon as my own dogs started barking, I tightened my grip instinctively on Maia's lead (fortuitously, I'd yet to take it off). Maia immediately flew forward and her strength was just too much for me. I slipped and fell and was dragged unceremoniously along the ground behind her, face down in the mud, my knee twisted to one side. Which hurt. But I knew I mustn't let go. By now someone had run across to grab the other dog, thank goodness, but I was still face down on the ground, unable to get up. What I really needed was to go to hospital, but first I had to somehow get my dogs safely home.

So, I compromised. I'd head home, albeit in absolute agony, and go to the GP on the way. 'What you really need to do,' my GP told me, is go to hospital. 'Oh, and by the way, you shouldn't be driving.'

Paqo volunteered to drive, but I politely declined. I also refused to do as I was told – hospital could wait. Instead, with some difficulty and a lot of swearing I managed to drive the rest of the way home, stopping on the way at Waitrose for some self-medication. By hoisting myself up slightly on the handle, I could scoot round behind a trolley, so I scooted round to the wine aisle and chose a lovely red. That was what I wanted: a large medicinal glass of red.

Needless to say, the hospital was unimpressed when I finally made it into A&E the next morning. As I had already expected, I had torn a lot of ligaments and to my dismay they prescribed painkillers and complete rest. But how could I rest? I had dogs that needed walking! Yes, I had a garden, but if I didn't take them out and walk them, they'd be climbing the walls. And so, had I been able to, would I (ADHD does not do rest).

So, Wendy at Wood Green got an urgent message: *Please help. I have hurt myself and need to know more about what to do with dogs that have less exercise.* I then added multiple exclamation marks for good measure.

She saw it and she agreed to see us. Help was finally at hand and paw. I was also stunned when a rescue dog friend, Hilary, offered to help support the dogs' training. Without Wendy and Hilary, I'm genuinely not sure we would have been able to stay together.

I didn't yet know it, but (thanks also in part to Maia) I'd arrived at another life-changing moment.

CHAPTER 10

Ants in His Pants

Wendy terrified me at first. I was completely in awe of her and extremely anxious about doing well. Also, I was very nervous about my communication troubles. Suppose I got frustrated and said something harsh and unwittingly offended her – this woman whom I so admired and who had so generously agreed to help me – and completely blew it?

In the event, early on, it was the other way around, because a couple of sessions in Wendy mentioned in passing that it might be better if my voice was a little softer. I was really upset by this. My voice was me, I couldn't help how it sounded. Yes, I could speak softly when necessary – caring for a terrified Summer in Romania, for instance – but in my day-to-day life, I wasn't a naturally quiet person. Besides, the dogs were used to the way I spoke. I was who I was and the suggestion that I needed to change myself cut me to the quick. Because that was how I perceived Wendy's comment – that yet again, in yet another way, I wasn't good enough.

This kind of over-thinking was, and still is, my reality, the feeling of not being good enough always lurking in the shadows and, when triggered, putting me immediately on the defensive. Something would be said or implied and I'd get really upset. Criticism can wound me deeply – I take it so much to heart. So much so that it makes me feel as if I'm physically shrinking. It takes me straight back to being a child and being told I was no good by my mother. And all I want to do is walk away. It's a kind of self-sabotage, because it means there's no opportunity to put anything right.

I so nearly walked that day but having Wendy in my life was just way too precious a thing to give up on. So, screwing up my courage, I dug deep and told her how I felt. That I'd found what she'd said to me hurtful.

Wendy was mortified when I told her that and immediately apologetic. That was huge for me. First, because I'd done something which for me was extraordinary. For once I had stood up for myself and with calmness and dignity. Even more extraordinarily, she had listened – I had been *heard*. It was truly revelatory. A major lesson for me and a turning point in our fledgling relationship.

After our initial appraisal, we began travelling to Wood Green Rehoming Centre in Godmanchester for one-hour weekly lessons. It was a vast place, with different areas for all the different animals they rescued – as well as dogs and cats, they rehome chickens, goats, rabbits and rodents. They also provide support and expert advice for pet owners, including workshops and puppy training classes.

To which, it was soon clear, there was no point in taking Maia and Paqo. Maia had zero interest in doing training and though Paqo came with us for the first couple of sessions, he was happier wombling around with his beloved wolf lady back at home. It was the two youngsters that were really in need of some direction: Raffy because he could so easily become even more troubled without an intervention and Kratu ... Well, Kratu was Kratu: headstrong, impulsive, intelligent and assertive. All qualities that needed channelling in the right direction.

Kratu had ants in his hairy pants so the first thing Wendy wanted him to do – the foundation for all that was to come – was simply to learn to sit still. Which was, to me, rather familiar. Much as he and I were polar opposites in social situations, in this perpetual restlessness we were two of a kind. I'm not sure which one of us had the most restless legs so one of the first things we *both* had to accomplish was the tedious but necessary business of accompanying Wendy around the grounds of the centre and basically being still while she chatted to fellow staff members. Of course, as far as Wendy was concerned, it was Kratu who was learning this skill but I'm sure we were probably pulling exactly the same grimaces while desperately trying to control our fidgets.

Another thing we practised over and over early on was leaving Kratu in a room with Wendy when I went into the bathroom, so he'd learn to wait calmly for, and trust in, my return. A third involved entering the treasure trove that was the charity's on-site shop, where he had to learn to have good manners around the tempting array of toys and treats all around him. Kratu was always brilliant at this for a while, as if lulling me into a false sense of security, until the point where he could either no longer control himself and/or sensed my eye was off the ball. I suspect the latter. He would then do a quick smash-and-grab raid, seizing a mouthful of whatever was closest. Needless to say, I always had to buy his ill-gotten gains, which he'd release to me on command, knowing that he wouldn't see them again until we'd finished that day's training.

Kratu learned very quickly (much faster than Raffy, who learned at his own leisurely pace). He would learn to do something after only two or three repetitions, then do a big play bow with his bearbum in the air. Then he'd bark at me, his message clear: *That's it, I'm done here.* And he'd mean it. He had a very short attention span and he was defiant and strong-willed with it, so sometimes he'd jump up to investigate the window ledge where they kept the toys, in search of one to steal, and other times he'd refuse to engage with any training other than the two or three tricks he currently favoured.

He was also emerging as a dog who enjoyed being the centre of attention – he loved playing the clown and people's laughter fuelled his comedy routines. Not all dogs like being laughed at, but Kratu positively thrived on it. He was never happier than when he knew all eyes were on him and he could put on a bit of a show.

I looked forward to my teacher time too. Wendy, in my mind, soon became 'Wendy the Teacher,' and, diligent student that I was, I respected her greatly. Well, except when I wanted to do things my own way which, ever patient, she took with good grace.

She was getting to know me so well. That too was revelatory; how she understood me, how she read me. One day, when I was talking about Kratu's short attention span, she told me that he wasn't so different from his owner. She pointed out that when I didn't grasp something in ten to twenty seconds, I would also switch off and change the direction of the conversation, to 'Ooh, look at this, Wendy. We learned a new trick last night – watch!'

So that was me told. She definitely had double trouble on her hands, dog and owner equally loud and impulsive. But, my goodness, I was keen to learn. The proverbial sponge. We'd practise what we learned in class every single day, so keen were both of us to have progress to show her. Not long, laborious sessions, we kept it short and kept it fun – something I soon learned was key to success. A couple of minutes at regular intervals throughout the day, always ending on a positive note and a reward so the dog looked forward to the next session with enthusiasm.

Learning basic social manners, heel work and impulse control were all precursors to the more advanced training methods. Of which there were, I was coming to realise, an astonishing amount. The more I learned, the more I realised there was *to* learn. And there were myriad ways to go about it too. Wendy taught a method of training based on naming and explaining, known as SATS (Syn Alia Training System). We then added a training regime called Do As I Do, a method developed by an Italian scientist, Claudia Fugazza, which really resonated with me as it was all about copying, something that had been such a powerful survival tool for me.

It was a combination that proved the right one for Kratu as well and meant that within a few weeks, we could dispense with 'shaping', a common method of behaviour training which involves first breaking everything down into simple steps. It takes a long time and it was of no surprise to anyone that I found it spectacularly boring.

Kratu's thirst to learn meant he steamed ahead too. He loved learning and was developing a great sense of humour. I had taught him, Raffy and Paqo to ring a bell I'd hung on the end of a string attached to a door handle. One day I was in my bedroom and I heard the bell ring. I went to investigate to find Kratu smacking it with his paw to see if he would get an extra treat for random ringing. Needless to say, the combination of cheek, ingenuity and genius meant he got several ...

Given how keen he was to learn, I also taught him another trick I'd seen. I would do a pretend sneeze and say 'atishoo!' and taught him to pull a tissue out of the box in his teeth and hand it to me. He loved learning this and picked it up almost immediately, though Kratu being Kratu, he soon went freestyle. His version, which was obviously a great deal more fun, was to pull out one tissue from the box, then another, then another – in fact, he didn't stop whipping tissues from the box, frenetically and with great glee, till the entire box was empty.

I laughed until my stomach ached, in a snowstorm of flying Kleenex. And learned something too: that my laughter was what helped him pick up things so quickly, something that I learned was called 'marking a behaviour'. My laughter was the same as getting a treat – it rewarded him in the same way as a food item.

Though there was no running away with the idea that training Kratu was easy, not back in those early days, because if his attention wandered so too would he, running off to investigate anything that took his fancy and invariably sticking his nose in where he shouldn't be. He'd also bark when I asked things – the canine equivalent of being cheeky and answering back. Wendy tackled this by asking me to leave when he became opinionated or overexcited; I was only to return and resume training when he was calm again. Some days I felt like the cuckoo in a cuckoo clock, I was in and out of that door so many times.

I learned a valuable lesson there too. That these fundamental and important things take a *lot* of time and patience, but if you want to achieve them then you mustn't give up. Almost all dogs and their trainers get there eventually, and eventually we did.

Manners don't just make man, they make happy dogs and owners. So as winter gave way to spring, we did more and more outside, walking endlessly round all the large open paths at the centre, plus in and out of all the buildings (the workspace, the shop of many temptations, the offices), reinforcing happy-calm as opposed to happy launching.

Raffy too continued to improve. He was intelligent, but he used his intelligence differently. Where Kratu would pick something up really quickly, Raffy liked to ponder. And ponder, and ponder ... Progress, but at the sort of tortoise-like pace that for someone like me, with my ADHD, sometimes felt like walking through melted tar on a hot day.

An hour of unbroken training is a lot, especially for dogs with a short attention span, so I'd give them turns, getting one out to play while the other one rested, which meant both could learn one-to-one and at their own pace. And though Raffy's anxiety at entering some of the buildings seemed to tell its own unhappy story, his fear began abating and he learned his first trick, 'shy': when I said the word, he'd lower his head and place a paw over his eyes. He charms people with that one to this day.

Kratu, meanwhile, was piling on skill after skill, learning trick after trick, such as putting his paws on objects, displaying his intelligence by quickly learning which paw was which. Then came 'bum bum', where I trained him to put his bottom down on command and he still does that – on people, chairs, anywhere he can fit his big hairy bearbum. He plonks it down with a great flourish and grins. As much as any dog can grin, Kratu does. It never ceases to fill me with joy.

In short, we were observing a simple truth in action: if you put in the work, you get the results. Within three months of beginning our sessions with Wendy, Raffy had grown in confidence and Kratu was progressing at an astonishing rate.

And I was showing signs of progress too. For the first time in years my life was almost filled to bursting and with what I loved best, which was hard work and routine. Caring for my dogs had now overtaken almost everything else: their training, their welfare, their exercise and diet. Which left little time available for introspection and anxiety. It was as if Kratu had pushed open a door for me and beyond that was light. The light of a happier, more fulfilling and more peaceful life.

All little Tess and I had to do now was step through it.

CHAPTER 11

'That One's a Rum 'Un.'

As winter turned to spring and the first green shoots started appearing in the wilderness of my new garden, I began feeling green shoots of hope inside me too. I was starting to settle in and had struck up a real friendship with my neighbour, Colin. He had grown to really love the dogs and I had already invited him on a couple of walks with us. When he suggested he might take Paqo out from time to time *for* me, I'd agreed and he was now doing so regularly.

Paqo was the easiest of my dogs at this time. He was well behaved and calm – lovely to walk on the lead – and as long as he was never taken off-lead, I had no concerns. Colin knew not to do that, so when he didn't arrive back from a walk one day, I was naturally worried – what could have happened to them? Colin had lived in the area for years, so it seemed inconceivable that he'd be lost.

After an hour had passed, I was beginning to be seriously concerned. Colin wasn't a youngster – could he perhaps have had a fall? I jumped in the car and drove around for a good twenty minutes, but there was no sign of them anywhere. But perhaps there wouldn't be – much of where we walked the dogs was off-road. I returned home. Maybe they'd already be there.

It was almost another half hour later when they finally appeared, Paqo looking tired but otherwise fine, and poor Colin frazzled, hot and exhausted.

'Are you okay?' I asked, anxious to see him in such a state.

He shook his head, but only slightly, not one to emote. 'That one's a rum 'un,' he said.

It turned out that Paqo had seen a partridge. Pheasants he liked, but partridges he liked to chase. I have no idea to this day what he has against partridges but he had apparently slipped his collar, set off in hot pursuit and led Colin, a man in his late sixties, a merry dance around a muddy field for over an hour, before finally sitting down and waiting for Colin to go and catch him, evidently bored or tired or both.

I was laughing by the time Colin finished recounting his story. I couldn't help it, and neither, now the debacle was done with, could he. But I wondered: *did* he slip the lead or did my neighbour, in a fit of misplaced confidence, let him off himself? I didn't press it. If he had, there was no chance he'd do so again, anyway.

'Still,' I told him, trying hard not to giggle, while Paqo snored blissfully in his bed, 'good bit of exercise for you both. Good to stay fit, Colin. Keeps you younger for longer!'

Both rum 'uns, the pair of them.

Training, meanwhile, was gathering pace. And since Kratu in particular was making such good progress, and Wendy already knew I wanted to do so much more with him, she suggested that between lessons I stepped up his socialisation by regularly taking him to places where there'd be lots of distractions, even more than he experienced on our walks around Ely and the couple of dog shows we'd attended when he was smaller.

'Something busier,' she suggested, like a big county show or something. It'll give you a chance to practise his heel work with distractions.'

Training with distractions is an important part of the process, then comes duration, then distance – the three 'D's of training. So, this would be a good start, but for me such an outing would be extremely challenging. I had become very reclusive, living my rural way of life, and to be thrust into such a situation would be hard. Walking around town there would always be an option to escape any crowds of people, but a big show would see hundreds, perhaps thousands of them, corralled in a small space. Plus, people at shows behaved differently than in the street – they'd drift around aimlessly, be distracted themselves, plus all the families, the children running around everywhere, the noise … Just thinking about it filled me with dread. But something else too: resolve and determination. If this was what it took, then bring it on! Which was why, a couple of weeks later, in April 2015, I ventured to Suffolk and a comedy of errors soon ensued.

I decided to take both Raffy and Kratu – my once wayward teens – and had sensibly (or so I thought) brought plenty of roast chicken as high-reward, tempting treats and co-opted a helper in the shape of Anya, a young girl I'd got to know via the pet shop I used, and whom Kratu adored. Every time he went in the shop, she would come straight over to greet him and sit on the floor, so he could plonk himself down onto her lap amid mutual squeals of delight.

We set off with me full of that resolve I just mentioned. As soon as we arrived, I had a growing sense of uncertainty. The show – All About Dogs – was enormous. There were crowds and crowds of people and the parking was horrendous. So many people, and so many cars; how on earth was I going to find my way in? I cast around vainly – I couldn't even see any entrances.

It was no better when I did finally find my way into the showground. I had to find the Kennel Club Scruffts arena (Scruffts is a competition purely for crossbreeds) but it was like trying to find a needle in a haystack – the place was just so vast and also teeming with people. By the time we'd made it far enough to enter the dogs in a couple of categories, I was feeling anxious and distracted. In contrast, Kratu's excitement was evident. He also knew my mind was elsewhere and he took full advantage; he was much more interested in what was going on around him than listening to me.

We got through the classes somehow, though not without incident. Kratu was getting bored and wanted out, back into the human and canine throng and the fun that could be found there. I hadn't realised how long it took for the judges to go around everyone and I fear I switched off a bit too. I'd also let Anya hold Kratu, as he liked her so much, foolishly thinking her more capable than she was, forgetting that her own dog was a pug, not a huge hairy powerhouse like Kratu, so I stood next to her in the arena so I could help her if need be.

I was right to. When it came to Kratu's turn before the steely-looking Kennel Club judge, instead of standing quietly, Kratu immediately threw himself onto the grass, wiggling and squiggling like a two-year-old having a tantrum. She looked mightily displeased at this, but worse was to come. As I silently willed him to stop it and stand up, he pulled his back legs in close to his stomach and let out a double bunny kick of such incredible force that it nearly knocked her clean off her feet.

I watched, horrified – it was as if it was happening in slow motion – as she keeled forward, her face only inches from hitting the ground before she managed to put her arms out and recover her balance. I also had to stifle a powerful urge to giggle; whether due to nerves or my unique sense of humour (probably both) it was my go-to behaviour in times of trouble. No place, no rosette, for naughty Kratu.

Raffy fared better. He won third place in Most Handsome Male, which, of course, meant a trip into the middle of the show ring for him to claim his rosette and our prize of a photo call with the judge.

I took him, leaving Anya holding Kratu at the edge, but just as I was about to do my smile for the camera, I spotted a streak of hairy grey lightning. Kratu had slipped his lead and was charging towards to me at great speed, screeching to a halt in front of me, evidently very pleased that he'd photobombed his brother.

The judge lunged for Kratu's lead, her face a picture of fury. 'GIVE me THAT DOG!' she spat out as she grabbed it. I half expected to see steam coming out of her ears. Some judges had zero sense of humour, I was learning. And I've learned a lesson too, I thought irritably, as Raffy's picture was taken. That Kratu should practise his bunny kicks so they're even more effective.

There was another, more serious lesson to be learned though: that I was the only one to handle Kratu and that teenagers would be teenagers – they have a lot of energy. Energy that in Kratu's case simply wouldn't be contained. And, despite agreeing with his sentiments (if not his bunny-kicking inaccuracy), we clearly needed to get back to the drawing board. His heel work was wonderful, he just needed to contain himself in the moment and particularly in a show ring. So more work and back to the basics. We resumed training with a vengeance.

Got to be honest, though: I did find it funny.

I was still involved in rescuing dogs from Romania at this time, but becoming increasingly angry and disillusioned. Now I knew more about some of the things that were going on, I couldn't help but be suspicious and concerned. I was also anxious to make people aware of the pitfalls, posting regularly on Facebook to try to help them wise up, posting warnings on social media, reminding them not to automatically trust in rescue back-up; to find out if it was really in place, because if it wasn't then they were going to be in trouble – as would the dogs people had gone to such lengths to rescue and find happy homes for in the UK.

What was upsetting though was that people didn't seem interested, many blithely carrying on like before. Many dogs were still coming into the UK and getting 'lost', some returning to rescue, the supposed rescue back-up non-existent, while others would be advertised on sites like Gumtree. Dogs would manage to escape from badly fenced gardens (the natural urge of a dog used to freedom on the streets, when suddenly contained within a house, is to flee). A few, not having been spayed or neutered, had produced puppies; the very situation they had supposedly escaped from in Romania was now happening anyway, just in the UK.

In the end, it still came down to money – money being exchanged for the dogs, in the form of 'adoption fees', with the guilty parties, both in Romania and the UK, more interested in the ever-increasing sums involved than the continued safety and wellbeing of the poor dogs. Rescue needed – still needs – a big welfare shake-up.

So, unable to change much, and saddened at people's reluctance to accept the truth, I turned my attention increasingly to just my own dogs: at least for them, I would do all I could to ensure their happiness, health and wellbeing. Concentrating on my own dogs was a joy and a revelation. There was so much to learn and I wanted to learn all of it, and so we practised as diligently as ever.

I learned about rewards and how to deploy them. How truly high-value rewards could be used for doing really good work. Roast chicken was mine (I would scour supermarkets for end-of-day, end-of-shelf-life bargains for my freezer), but only to be used sparingly. Everyday treats were supposed to be little bits of cheese and ham, or bought ones with natural ingredients. High-reward treats were often sausages. Sometimes I also used lamb's liver, cooked and chopped finely – rewards only needing to be minuscule. (Poor Wendy didn't like the smell of liver and could never help a slight grimace when I pulled my trusty bag out. It always made me smile.)

I also learned about 'jackpots' – when a dog does something so amazing that they get a succession of treats as a reward. You beam with delight and say 'Jackpot!' in your best happy voice. Kratu adored jackpots, and he couldn't gobble them up fast enough. Not the first time I would see him 'smile', his face lit up with joy. And it made *me* feel happy too. There was no doubt about it: bit by bit, my world was completely changing.

But it didn't all go smoothly. When it came to Kratu, since we were both strong-willed and determined, there were days when we couldn't make it click. And when that happened, there was no treat in the world that would work – he'd just wander off and ignore me.

Other times, his irrepressible nature got the better of him and was simply too much to be dampened. We were at a dog show one day and it was a slow one. Between classes I was a little bored and hungry and while walking Kratu to get a bacon roll, I saw they had a fastest-sausage-eating competition. So, to kill time, after my snack, I paid my pound for him to enter.

The course was simple: the dogs had to stand at the start line, then run down a line of poles, each of which had a piece of sausage on a plate at the bottom. There were ten poles and when the dog had reached the last one, they had to race straight back to the beginning. Their speed at doing this would be timed. Pretty simple.

Kratu loves sausages, so it's no surprise that he was eyeing them up. He could see them, and smell them, and I egged him on a bit too saying, 'Sooooosages, Kratu! Ready steady go!'

Gobbling them up, he was ecstatic. He made it to the end and raced back, past the finish line and on, right up to the judge … who happened to be holding the Tupperware container holding the rest of the competition sausages. He then launched through the air with amazing precision and managed to knock it out of her hands. As soon as the container hit the ground, he wrestled with the lid and ripped it open, then stuck in his head and grabbed a mouthful of sausages – so many that, as he re-emerged with his self-awarded prize, sausages were spilling out of the sides of his mouth as he munched away in happy oblivion.

I was mortified, but at the same time I couldn't stop laughing and when I start giggling, I go all weak and floppy – in no fit state to extract his head from the box. I just about managed, and by now people all around were laughing too.

After that I retreated to a safe distance to watch the other competitors but my competitive nature got the better of me. And as I knew Kratu would love it too, I paid another pound so that he could have another go.

We had to wait our turn then for another dog in front of us: a brown chocolate Labrador, a breed notorious for their immense love of food. The judge had just put out more sausage pieces and he was sitting at the start line when out of nowhere came this huge streak of flying grey fur.

What?

I turned around and saw the empty collar hanging off the lead dangling in my hand.

No dog.

The escapee – yes, *my* dog – then launched himself at the Lab, knocking him sideways off the start line, before performing a rerun, charging down the line of plates, snaffling all the sausages he could stuff in his mouth, while the audience, the judge, the Lab's owner and me were all literally rolling around with laughter. Unsurprisingly, the innovative, self-rewarding, sausage-stealing dog I managed to catch was unrepentant and immensely pleased with himself.

Later on, after our show classes and because he'd had such fun, I took him back to the sausage-eating competition one last time as a special treat before going home. They had, however, run out of pork sausages by this time (perhaps, hmmm, due to earlier pilfering). All that remained were Linda McCartney vegetarian ones, causing Kratu to look at me with surprise and disgust.

'What's this?' he seemed to say. 'A non-sausage?'

We didn't win it, but what we did do is make a priceless memory. That is winning too – winning at life. Making moments and loving them.

But cocking things up, doing it wrong, was all part of the learning for me too. I'd report back to Wendy and we'd discuss what I'd done, and she'd explain how, invariably, it came down to me doing something incorrectly, or that I hadn't explained what was required well enough. She'd then put me on the right track and off we'd go again, getting better. And every step forward felt like such an achievement, motivation now coursing through my veins.

I had always shopped at charity shops – it was one of the main ways I amassed my wardrobe – but I visited them even more regularly now, rummaging among the toys as well as the tops and jeans, for things for Kratu to learn to touch on command, to hold between his paws, to push along, to sit on. If it squeaked, made any sort of noise, could be held or pushed along, I got it. And we had so much fun. Kratu really liked paw work. Already he'd learned the names and was now learning how to touch on command, with left paw, or right paw, back paws, paws on, paws off. He often got overenthusiastic and would bash something very hard, sometimes sending it into the air, which he loved. If I asked him to go and touch an object away from me – usually a little toy – he would run to it with great gusto, pounce on it like a cat on a mouse and then slap it into oblivion with a mighty paw whack. Kratu didn't do finesse, he was a paws-on, lust for life, larger-than-life, full-on character.

Kratu also loved to jump and could jump very high so I'd build jumps out of all sorts of garden paraphernalia. He jumped on and off straw bales, sailing up and through the sky, as I watched in joy and disbelief. He'd tackle ponds, if we encountered them, like a hovercraft, tucking his paws up and skimming across them effortlessly – he was a big hairy, magnificent, flying machine.

Doing all of that with him was like returning to pockets of joy I remembered so vividly from back in my childhood, putting jumps together for imaginary ponies back in my Black Beauty days. I rarely visited my past because it was usually too painful, but making those jumps, and remembering Black Beauty, was returning to a happier time. And the happiness I felt, however fleeting, was real.

But, at the same time, we were both deadly serious. In training my dogs, and in training *this* dog in particular, I was also, however odd it sounds, training myself. When you think about it, we both benefited greatly from this and I was beginning to learn that trying to guide the behaviour of an intelligent animal involves moulding your own alongside. First and foremost, I was regularly calming my natural tendency towards impulsiveness and impatience. Kratu and

I were twins with our impulsive behaviours and we both needed to learn how to curb it. Mine had got me in dangerous situations time after time. I had no idea why the urge to do something suddenly appeared inside me and why I would unquestioningly follow that thinking. Similarly, Kratu needed to restrain his natural urge to greet others by launching on them, to listen and engage with me, instead of doing exactly what he wanted.

So many times, when faced with frustration, my default had always been to walk away. Here, I couldn't do that and I realised I didn't want to. Instead, if Kratu couldn't do something I wanted him to, I would have to accept that I hadn't explained it correctly, think again and start over. That diligence, dedication and determination to see this through was all new. This was my life changing, and I was learning new skills all the time.

And I liked it. Other than the Andean, Toltec and other healing ways I had learned, I had never found anything so interesting. Or *fun* – something that, for me, was a distant and far-removed memory, because pain had wiped most of it away. Now pain was being pushed into the background and, feeling freer, I learned alongside Kratu, growing closer to him every day as we started to understand exactly what made the other tick, our bond deepening with every hour we spent working hard together.

When we allow dogs to be dogs and work *with* them, we can achieve a great deal, but only if we take the trouble to really try to understand their needs, learn their body language and help them to communicate with us. For me, that process of training and learning how to mutually communicate is what deepens that bond and that friendship. And though I wasn't at that time really consciously aware of it, it was also turning out to be the ultimate prescription for me – for not worrying so much about myself.

Redirection is an amazing dog training tool; redirecting undesirable behaviour towards something that *is* desirable. Subconsciously, I was learning to do this myself – and to great effect.

Another powerful tool for not engaging with my personal demons.

In early May 2015, I saw an advert on Facebook. They were looking for people to participate in an experiment for a Sky TV panel show called *Duck Quacks Don't Echo*. (In fact, this is a non-fact – they do!) The idea was to test the theory that when their owner looks into their eyes, speaks softly or strokes them, dogs produce more of the 'love' chemical, oxytocin.

Buoyed by the experience of Kratu's zest for performing, I did my usual impulsive thing and applied for the show. What I hadn't taken into account was when I acted impetuously like this, one of the *almost guaranteed* consequences would be that I'd end up producing way too much of another chemical – adrenalin. Why on earth did I keep doing this to myself?

As the day of the filming loomed I felt my anxiety increasing and the usual furious tussle going on in my brain. I didn't have to do it. If it all got too much, I could cancel. But I mustn't, I must not give in to the fear. And increasingly, I didn't. I'd actually come to look forward to the feeling of short-term euphoria that came with letting Kratu persuade me (I had absolutely no doubt he was behind it) to push myself beyond the boundaries I had always set myself.

But there was a problem. The experiments were being filmed in central London, which meant parking would be impossible, so I had no choice but to travel there by train. I struggle with public transport at the best of times and trains are a major trigger. Not just the trains, but the tracks. Especially the tracks, my fear of them stemming from a memory during a very dark time in my life when, without even properly registering what I was doing, I jumped down and sat on the rails in an underground station, on the point of giving up. Still, today, even the act of stepping from platform to train, of having to cross that void, is enough to send me straight back to that day. It's both a trigger and a memory – things you just can't stop from invading your brain. However, you can overcome them and that would be what I'd have to do, though I knew stepping over that gap from platform to train would be an act of huge courage and faith.

But I would be with Kratu, and I knew he would centre me. He'd calm me down, still my nerves, make me see things through his eyes – *this is fun, Mum! Don't worry! This is an adventure!* And though I knew it would be hard, I also knew I could trust him, just as he trusted me to prove to *him* that the world was as delightful a place as instinct usually told him.

The experiment was being filmed at a studio in East London and, on the face of it, looked fairly straightforward. We'd take a urine sample from our dogs to measure their oxytocin levels, then the director would ask us to show our dogs lots of affection. They'd then ask us to take a second sample and test that one too to see if more oxytocin was present.

Straightforward, that is, in theory, except for two words: *urine sample.* How on earth do you get a urine sample from a huge hairy dog? With a great deal of difficulty, I can tell you. There were around ten of us, plus our dogs, all of different breeds and sizes, and we were taken out into a central courtyard, dotted with hedges, the idea being that the dogs would naturally want to mark their space, allowing us to gather the precious liquid. Simple!

I was given a plastic pot that I was supposed to put underneath his wee stream, but Kratu has a hairy undercarriage so determining where the wee would come from was tricky. Plus, my head was upside down, which was making me dizzy, only adding to the difficulty. I got a lot over my hand as every time I moved towards the wee stream, he would be backwards eyeballing me and managing to step away to avoid having to have anything to do with this strange thing I seemed hell-bent on shoving under his willy.

It was also a reminder that Kratu is very, *very* strong, especially when his inquisitive nature kicks in. When we took the first wee sample to the table, and he decided that he wanted to be *on* it (the better to investigate what treats might be on there), he managed, to my embarrassment, to get his front paws up on the table, nearly knocking the rest of the samples on the floor.

It was classic Kratu, the action of a first-rate opportunist. Taking advantage of the fact that I was holding on to the wee sample so carefully that his lead was the last thing on my mind. Rapidly handing over the sample, I performed a hurried front end lift-off before chaos ensued and walked off with as much dignity as I could muster. And all on camera.

Thanks, Kratu, I thought, for the out-take.

After the oxytocin high came the inevitable low, as we were taken to the local park to do more filming. Which would have been fine, except the park was full of potential danger. Other dogs, small and large, several racing round the park off their leads, with no recall. Not to mention a few dog owners with attitude, whose attitude seemed to be that aggression in their dogs was a good thing.

Not good for me. I'd always kept Kratu's interactions with other dogs happy and controlled, it being important for him to learn that they were great to mix with. He's a big dog and if he got over-excited, he would be hard to hold on to.

I also had a natural fear because of the incident with Maia – we'd been in a park when that dog had latched on to her throat. So, no sooner had we got there than my mind was into overdrive – both with the anxiety of being in such an unpredictable situation and working out how I'd be able to keep Kratu safe from anyone with an out-of-control, reactive dog off-lead. I couldn't – and wouldn't – risk his good nature.

Happily, we got through the last bit of filming without incident, but where others lingered to chat, I said my farewells and hurried away. Though I felt a bit sad to be leaving, I was listening to my instincts, which were telling me to get the hell out of there.

Once on the way back to the station, the rigid control that had got us through the day soon dissipated, leaving me weak and a bit wobbly at the knees. Kratu came into his own then, as he would go on to do on countless occasions in the future, leading me back, leading me home, seeming to know the way instinctively. And I let him; on to the platform, on to the train and off again at the other end. I just followed his guidance and let him take me where I was told. When we finally reached the car, sitting in the dusk of the station car park, he turned and waited patiently for me to find my keys and unlock it.

All systems are go, Thunderbirds, I thought. Yes, m'lady.

That was me, I thought – Parker. I was Kratu's trusty chauffeur. It made me roar with laughter, the stress of the day melting away.

'I'm not wearing a cap though,' I told him.

The stress would return, I knew, but I could deal with it. Life comes with stress attached. And we had done it! Together, we had achieved something big. And though I swore never to put myself through anything like that again, it seemed Kratu had other ideas.

CHAPTER 12

A Natural Instinct

Despite the debacle at the All About Dogs show and the wee-experiment stresses, when, in June 2015, I saw an advert on Facebook for a Canine Supermodel competition being run by *Dogs Today* magazine, being a sucker for punishment, I immediately decided I should take Kratu and Raffy. They were beautiful dogs, after all.

The competition was being held as part of something called DogFest in Surrey. It was a bit of a drive, but I'd now gathered so much psychological momentum, I was keen to get out there and do more. I really believed in my dogs and had to learn to believe in myself too.

With around 18,000 people regularly attending, DogFest is one of the biggest shows in the UK. Having never been to anything like it before, though, I had no idea at that point just *how* big it was. Which was probably a plus, because if I had, I might never have found the courage. I was also anxious, as I always was, about all the other dogs who'd be there, especially those under less than full control by their owners, of which I knew there would definitely be a few.

I decided not to ask Anya, since she lacked the physical strength, but happily, Zoe, a friend of a friend, said she'd go along with me. We'd chatted a lot on Facebook and her own dog was a strong Staffie, and as she also did some dog walking, she knew enough about handling bigger dogs so I knew she could provide a capable pair of extra hands.

Zoe was young, though, which obviously comes with its own set of rules, and when I arrived at her place bright and early on the day of the show, there was no answer at the door and she wasn't picking up her phone.

Could I do this on my own? Yes, I told myself. I can. But did I want to put myself through all that stress on my own? No. I was so pissed off at that point that I nearly went home, but neither Kratu nor fate was having any of my nonsense and just at the point when I was about to drive off in a huff, Zoe appeared, looking very much the worse for wear, having been on something of a bender the night before.

So with me suffering my usual sensory overload, and Zoe with her hangover from hell, we mostly kept away from the vast and shifting hordes, the sheer volume of people and animals who'd be there having been something I had failed to take into account. Still, Kratu and Raffy couldn't help but turn heads and whenever they did, they set about charming everyone in their orbit, including one particularly beautiful lady whom we met at the Portaloos and who thought the pair of them were absolutely gorgeous.

But despite that, or perhaps because of it, I began to feel increasingly overwhelmed. This was a pretty major dog show and everyone seemed to be taking it *so* seriously, while in contrast, I felt very out of place. These were people I struggled to identify with too; they had bows and fancy coats on their dogs, all manner of other paraphernalia, and my anxiety levels just kept rising and rising as so many people seemed to be busier socialising than paying attention to what their pets might be getting up to, many of which were on extendable leads.

It was so exhausting trying to keep Kratu and Raffy both groomed and away from all the overexcited dogs that would come flying up out of nowhere, that after having entered four classes in which neither of them won anything, I reached the inescapable conclusion that they just didn't like my dogs and was all for giving up and leaving.

By this time I was feeling quite despondent, but since we'd already entered the supermodel competition, and not relishing the lengthy drive home, I decided we might as well stay for it. I wasn't interested in the main prize of three months' worth of dog food, but the other prize, the chance to have one of my dogs on the magazine's cover – confirmation, almost, that it wasn't just me who thought my beloved dogs were beautiful. That kind of validation meant a lot to me.

Tired and stressed, I was heading for a meltdown. It was a warm, blustery day and I'd chosen the wrong clothes, my shirt billowing around me like a tent in a tornado – it kept puffing up every time a breeze got underneath it and I felt like the Michelin Man. Not a good look and not the one I'd intended. I was also feeling increasingly sweaty and fed up as we walked around to where the competition was being held.

The supermodel competition was obviously the highlight of the day, with a huge array of dogs having been entered. It was being judged by a trio of women who were well known in the dog world. Michelle from Natural Instinct, the dog food company who'd sponsored the competition, Penel Malby, the photographer from

Dogs Today magazine, and its editor, Beverley Cuddy, who, mic in hand, had started talking about the highlights of the day.

By this time, I was shutting down, so I wasn't really listening – just looking at the vast array of dogs in the ring, some of whom were truly beautiful, so we obviously didn't have a hope in hell of winning. I only woke up when I heard Beverley say how two dogs had stood out all day for her and looked around: which two out of the impressive candidates might they be? It was then that I did a double take – it was the Portaloo lady! The Portaloo lady was the one doing the judging! And then, to my astonishment, I heard the name Raffy.

I was stunned: she'd said Raffy. The winner was my Raffy! It took a long moment for that to sink in. I then turned to Zoe: 'You take him in,' I told her. 'You've handled him all day.' So it was Zoe who walked him into the centre of the ring to meet Beverley, Michelle and Penel.

I was so proud at that moment. So incredibly proud. Standing there in the wind, looking on, in my stupid fashion-disaster tent-shirt, it struck me that I was here with my two Roma camp dogs and one of them had just won a national UK super-model competition. My oh my, oh my … I was completely lost for words.

My mind was in a blur, unable to take in what had just happened, as Michelle walked us over to the Natural Instinct stand, but she was so lovely, so warm and kind, that she soon put me at my ease – 'Oh, and it's actually a year's supply of food,' she told me. 'We changed it.'

A *year's* supply of food. Another sparkle added to the fairy tale as a constant worry, having taken on Raffy as well as Kratu, was how on earth was I going to afford to feed them. Such a generous gift would make a massive difference to me.

As Zoe and I left the show, I couldn't feel the ground beneath my feet – it really was as if I was walking on air. And while I relived every moment of the day I'd started off dreading, the supermodel and his brother slept the whole way home.

That day was the start of a completely different life for me. Not just from the life I'd started living when I first saw Hero looking out at me from Facebook, from the life I had lived before and perhaps the person I had always been.

Someone who had always been on the run.

Because something inside me had always run away. It had, or so I'd thought, been the only coping mechanism available to me. As a child, I had run away to the comfort of solitude and nature. I had run away as a teenager after the death of my father when I could no longer bear being at home. I had run from squat to squat, into danger, into serious drug addiction, when I couldn't find my place in the adult world. Over and over, I had run into dangerous places; bad situations, where my naivety and innocence were exploited, leading to violence and cruelty and abuse.

I'd been written off countless times and by so many people. And by myself when I made the painful decision about my daughter's future. I had run to drugs because they were so good at numbing my pain and then later, to the other side of the world, in search of myself and more meaning to my world. I had needed answers to so many things and gone in search of peace and calm and answers only to discover that all that running had got me nowhere.

I couldn't run away from my deeply flawed self.

Yet here I was, an older woman with her dogs and, by some miracle – it really felt like that – I had stopped running. I had stood still and looked at fear – always a few steps behind me, always causing me to keep running away. It was now time to face my old adversary and we were going to have it out, once and for all.

Fear could still cripple me, certainly. In crowds, in conversation with strangers and in the show ring. But with Kratu by my side, I overcame it. His belief in me, his staunch loyalty, the love he showed he felt for me – these were such powerful forces to help me vanquish that fear. He was my shield and my armour, and I felt – and became – stronger with him there. And each time I overcame fear, I beat it back a little further, a personal victory – as if *I* was winning, alongside my dogs. Which, by now, they were, over and over.

After DogFest, I joined all the Facebook groups advertising dog shows. We would go on to travel to all sorts – to companions shows, fun dog shows, you name it. If there was a dog show within driving distance, we would go to it. To Oxfordshire, to Essex, to Norfolk, to Suffolk. We went, we saw and Kratu and Raffy conquered. Sometimes I would even take all my dog family, setting off with my dog crates and treats, and we would win and win again. Maia was soon winning lots of veteran classes and also Prettiest Bitch, Crossbreed Bitch and Appealing Eyes. Kratu and Raffy would often storm several classes – the rescue classes, the crossbreed classes, the Most Handsome Male, the Best Trick. I would begin to take home not one rosette, but five or six, or more. Between eight and fourteen soon became our usual. On one memorable occasion, we even won twenty. Sometimes, if I had all the dogs, we would do a lot of classes so each dog had their day and their turn. It was important they all had some time with me.

And we had fun, something that had always been so lacking in my life. Little Tess, who had always had such fun with Caspar the pony, was having fun again now, with the dogs – I was increasingly feeling her presence. We'd win trophies and cups, and all sorts of prizes – boxes of treats, which I would pass on to the Wood Green charity for use in their outreach work and sacks of food, which I would donate to charities, as I raw feed my dogs (my belief being that raw feeding has multiple health benefits, and that more essential nutrients are found in a raw meat-based diet. They also do much smaller, firmer poos!).

Winning, I soon learned, was not without its downsides. Just as is the case in any competitive arena, success brought on jealousy and everything that went with it. The more I won, it seemed, the more people disliked me and my dogs. Not all people, not even a majority of them, but just a few, whom I thought of as the dog show mafia – small groups that were gossipy, bitchy and spiteful.

I began to receive unkind and sometimes downright nasty comments. Some on social media and others face to face or within earshot at shows. Some I heard second-hand, giving me no right of reply. Things said about me, based on untruths and those good old green-eyed monsters. It hurt me. A lot. And, on more than one occasion, when one of my dogs' names was called out at a show as the winner, I actually heard people booing me.

'Oh God,' I overheard someone say at a show one day, 'it's that woman and her fucking Romanians.'

Now that was it for me, that really stuck. But not in the way they'd perhaps intended. Because I'd faced and overcome so much worse. So a group of spiteful people could not, and would not, touch me. I hate bullies, always have. Bullying is hateful and wrong. And nothing they could say or do would ever take me down. I knew I had done nothing wrong and I was proud of what I *had* done. I had worked bloody hard. My dogs had worked bloody hard. We had every right to exist and every right to win rosettes. For the first time in my life I was going to stand up for what I believed in: my dogs *and* myself.

The Four Agreements, based on the ancient Toltec wisdoms, is a code of conduct for living that I aspire to. They are:

Be impeccable with your word
Don't take anything personally
Don't make assumptions
Always do your best.

My sense of not being good enough meant I'd always struggled with the second one – taking things personally was for me almost second nature. But since Kratu had come into my life a change had come over me, a *good* change. I'd experienced so many sticks and stones in my life, there was no way I was going to let others' words hurt me.

I would, I resolved, take it on the chin – I'd taken far worse. They were not going to stop me or stand in my way. We were going to carry on winning – 'That woman and her fucking Romanians' were going nowhere.

CHAPTER 13

Mastery of Movement

Cinder Tess was going to the ball! Well, actually, to a music festival at the University of Surrey. Called One Live, it was conceived by the celebrity vet Noel Fitzpatrick, and the invitation had come from Michelle at Natural Instinct, who were sponsoring the event, to join them for a glass or two of champagne. From a personal standpoint, that meant a lot to me so nothing, my own anxieties included, was going to stop me from attending.

It had been a whirlwind couple of months. Shortly after DogFest, I'd travelled down to Penel Malby's home in Tadworth, Surrey, to do the photo shoot for Raffy's cover on *Dogs Today*. I'd been particularly nervous because it meant travelling halfway round the M25 and being stuck in traffic on that particular motorway was a bit like staying at Hotel California: once you checked in (well, on), it really did feel as if you could never leave.

Penel's studio was in her house and she immediately put me at my ease. She was so lovely, in fact – professional, patient and incredibly kind – that the experience turned out to be almost the opposite of my expectations. Raffy loved every second and Penel loved Raffy. She got some brilliant shots and I came away realising it was something I enjoyed too, another unexpected revelation. Could my dogs become *actual* supermodels? Kratu, especially, loved to pose – it came so naturally to him. He was already a supermodel in the making so it was definitely food for thought.

I wasn't just invited to the concert, however. I also had another very special appointment that day, at a big celebrity dog show called Pup Aid – I'd spotted a post on Facebook a few weeks before.

Founded by the TV vet Marc Abraham (aka 'Marc the Vet'), Pup Aid is a charity committed to ending puppy farming and educating the public about the right way to acquire a dog or puppy, be it via rescue or from a responsible breeder. As well as fundraising, the event was also about raising awareness, so they were looking for people who had their own puppy farming stories to tell.

This was of immediate interest to me because Tutty had certainly been puppy-farmed. Every season a new litter, kept in terrible conditions – and obviously in terrible condition herself, starving and beaten as she was. But still, two of her puppies, my gorgeous boys, had such wonderful temperaments and were growing up to be well-mannered, intelligent, happy dogs. Not your average dogs, no, but then I was not your average owner. They say you call in the dogs you need, don't they? Well, I had called in a wolfy one and these ancient heritage breed crosses. They were perfect for me. We were all a little bit wild, with big hearts. Together, as a family and a team, we worked.

I knew Pup Aid, as in the dog show, was a star-studded affair. Famous faces, famous judges and famous dog owners abounded; it was like a dog-themed who's who. As such, it was definitely not my thing. I'm terrible at recognising faces, for one thing, even those of people I know, and for another, I don't know who most celebrities are in the first place as I so rarely watch anything they're seen on. Celebrities also tend to draw huge crowds, of course – another thing that's definitely not for me. However, speaking up against abuse and raising awareness for rescue dogs and puppy farming *was* my thing, obviously, so I contacted a researcher who was helping with Pup Aid, and told her about Tutty, Kratu and Raffy, and was invited to take them along to the event and to have their stories told.

Now all I had to do was get myself organised. The show was being held at a big outdoor site in Primrose Hill in London, which meant the usual stress of driving down and finding somewhere to park as there wasn't any on-site parking available. I decided to enlist the help of my friend Ergun.

I'd met Ergun in London, back when Maia was a puppy, as he was a friend of my then neighbour. A former engineer of Turkish descent, he was now in his fifties with a white goatee beard and moustache. To my constant amusement, his facial hair wasn't dissimilar to Raffy's, so they made a good pair. Ergun loved dogs and had got to know all of mine well, befriending each new family member as they'd joined me. He was capable of walking them safely (no small thing in itself) and, apart from Casey, was the only person I completely trusted to dog-sit if I had to go away.

Ergun adored all my dogs and they adored him in return. When he came to stay, always sleeping in the dogs' room so I couldn't hear his snoring, they would join him in a cacophony of deep rumbling belly snores. (He, Raffy and Paqo would often share a bed and my goodness, could the three of them snore! I'm not sure which one was the loudest or how they didn't ever wake one another up.) Anyway, Ergun still lived in London and I knew it would be a fun day out for him.

I woke up on the day feeling achey and unwell, having picked up a bad cold from somewhere. It was becoming tedious, this apparent susceptibility to endless bugs. Could fear manifest into physical illness? It was certainly looking that way for me. I managed to find a parking space and Ergun met me at a café at the top of Primrose Hill, where I treated him to falafel wraps for lunch.

I'd decided I would handle Kratu and Ergun would handle Raffy, who was still entire at this point. Large breed dogs shouldn't be neutered too early as it can affect their growth plates – the regions of cartilage that sit at the end of the long bones of the legs and are responsible for healthy bone development. It's also beneficial for a male puppy who lacks confidence to remain entire for as long as possible; they need all the testosterone they can get.

Today, though, was already looking like being the day in which the decision to castrate him would be made for me. Raffy, it was clear, no longer lacked confidence. To my annoyance, he was swaggering around full of teenage testosterone, grumbling under his breath as he puffed out his macho chest while we circled around the show, me building myself up to be buoyant, charming and in control when I felt like I had as much backbone as soggy spaghetti. There was a long day in prospect with Medallion Man Raffy and his bloody balls would see it turn into a longer one – nuts off as soon as I could afford it!

If you go to a dog show you normally enter a few classes, so as I knew numbers would be restricted, our first job was to go and register. I chose Most Handsome Male for Raffy, Best Rescue for both of them and then, for fun, 'Dog Who Looks Most Like Their Owner'. That done, it was time to enter the fray.

I knew the show would be big, but there were even more people than I'd expected. It was an eclectic mix too, from fashionistas to children of all ages, to OAPs, to the usual sprinkling of eccentric types that I dubbed the 'dog show dandies', who'd attend all the big shows with their dogs, often dressed in matching outfits. You name it, they were all there, along with all the celebrities that I probably should have recognised and didn't.

As we'd been invited because they were going to tell Tutty's story, I had a pass to the VIP area. But the pass was just for me, which would mean leaving Ergun. And had I even wanted to, I knew I wouldn't feel comfortable in the little cordoned-off area with Macho Man Raffy and Kratu anyway. So friendship and safety were the order of the day and we stayed in our favourite little place, slightly away from the crowds. It also meant I could catch up with a couple of familiar faces: Sabine, a Facebook friend and former athlete, who was tiny perfection, and Sharon Rose, whom I talked to a lot on Facebook too and was instantly recognisable beside her huge grey Great Dane. Both wonderful women, it was calming to touch base with them.

The day unfolded in the usual accelerated whirlwind. I was feeling rough and overwhelmed and Kratu was quick to push his boundaries, his old honey monster behaviour creeping in. Raffy, too, was still mumbling and grumping under his breath and being donkey-like in his responses to all he was asked. Why on earth had I thought this was a good idea?

The first class we entered was Most Handsome, by which time I'd sent Ergun and Kratu back to my car for a quick break – it would be a long day and I didn't want to tire Ergun out, especially as he'd been so kind in offering to drive me to the concert later.

I walked across to the show ring with Raffy, keeping an eye out for anyone else I might know, thinking I must look for more people I knew on Facebook and say hello in person. With the shifting sea of faces beginning to blur, I couldn't see the wood for the trees. But it seemed our fortunes were about to change: Raffy came second!

Despite his cover model status, I was genuinely taken aback because there were so many beautiful dogs there, of all breeds and all shapes and sizes. And the prizes were wonderful too – we were given a carrier bag full of all sorts of treats, for both owner and dog, some of which I'd be able to regift to Wood Green.

Next up for us was Best Rescue and though Ergun had returned by now, I could see he was feeling the strain, Kratu having come back down from his enforced absence in a real mood. How dare anyone take him away from such a wonderful day! So many dogs, smells, people and fun! Ergun told me he had encountered a force and a strength that he'd not realised Kratu possessed.

This was hardly news – often people don't realise how physically strong my dogs are, because I've trained them to walk to heel and have good manners and grace, which makes it all look easier than it is. Which it often isn't. Raffy was behaving like a Stormin' Norman now as well, so it was fortunate that I spotted Jayne Boss. I knew Jayne because she'd fostered Gabby, Raffy's sister, and had found her a wonderful home. She was also the founder of a charity called German Shepherd Dog Rescue – they had a stall there – and since she was on hand and obviously used to handling lots of big dogs, I asked her if she'd handle Raffy for me. It was a huge class and I knew there would be a lot of standing around waiting; it was important the dogs stood still and behaved themselves.

Best Rescue was being judged by a number of celebrities, including Rachel Riley from the TV show *Countdown*, and her partner, *Strictly* professional dancer, Pasha Kovalev, who were allocated to our half of the entrants. Like many a *Strictly* fan before him, Raffy was so taken with the celebrated dancer that he couldn't help but express his devotion. Which, to my horror, involved him poking his nose beneath Pasha's crotch and taking a long, appreciative sniff. Not the kind of greeting the poor man was used to, I'm sure – or, come to think of it, he's much loved, so perhaps it is!

Kratu then went into overdrive, charming Rachel with a smouldering gaze and a swivel of the hips so he could lower his bearbum to the grass and sit gazing adoringly up at her. She was smitten, I could see, and evidently, so too was he. What a charmer! And clearly determined not to be outdone by his brother.

There were many entries and some genuinely heart-rending stories. As I listened, I grew increasingly convinced that we did not stand a chance of winning. And not just because of the genuine stories, some of which were very moving, but also because of the embellishers.

By now, I had come across embellishers at many dog shows – the large minority who, in their ambition to win, think nothing of playing fast and loose with the truth. In some cases, it was slight – just an exaggeration of the facts. But in others, the fabrications were nothing short of outrageous. On one occasion I'd even been at the same show as someone who'd copied Raffy's story about the tail cutting. Yes, cutting tails was common, but then I found out that the dog hadn't even come from Romania – it was just a normal rescue from a well-known UK shelter.

Sadly, these characters are everywhere and it was eye-opening to realise the lengths they would go to for a bag of prizes and a winner's rosette. But it turned out this wasn't to be their day. Raffy and Kratu had delighted Rachel and Pasha so much that, incredibly, they had decided to award them joint first place.

So it was me and Ergun dashing back up Primrose Hill with the Best Rescue prizes that afternoon, then the day spooled out in the way dog shows tend to everywhere. We were interviewed by a TV programme, where I was tongue-tied with exhaustion and the boys, finally behaving themselves, sat and posed for countless photos. People came and went; I met the talented photographer, Julia Claxton, who took all the official photos, and Victoria Featherstone Pearce, the beautiful former model who'd set up the rescue group K-9 Angels, and we spoke for some time about Kratu and Romanian rescue.

Meeting Victoria, in particular, was a real pick-me-up. She was as beautiful on the inside as she was on the outside and to spend time with someone with whom I felt so instantly comfortable provided a much-needed lift.

I saw someone else too, though only from afar. Her name was Lisa Garner and she was another well-known animal advocate. Also beautiful. Also glamorous. Also someone I'd have liked to meet, but I felt too shy and, by this time, too dishevelled to say hello.

It was once again into the limelight soon after though with the class 'Dog Who Looks Like Their Owner'. I still thought Ergun and Raffy stood a great chance, but since both had declined (the former rather firmly), it was left to me and Kratu. Lots of people go to town for fun classes like these, doing all they can to make themselves and their pets indistinguishable. With little money, and even less inclination to don fancy dress, I winged it, taking my hair out of its ponytail and shaking my head upside down. Now transformed, in that respect we really *were* indistinguishable: shaggy scruffy dog and shaggy scruffy owner, both with the same golden, blonde and (okay, if we *must*) grey hair. And the natural look went down a treat – we came second!

Another bag of goodies. Our stash was growing.

By now I was drifting off into my own world, however, so it was only seeing the announcer in the ring, mic in hand as she told Tutty's story, that made me realise I needed to get in there with her pronto – so that people could see, as well has hear about these boys, their puppy-farmed mum and the outcome.

Once that was done, I was exhausted, both mentally and physically. But there was still the Best in Show parade to come. This one – the finale – was being judged by Peter Egan, a well-known British actor and huge animal advocate. He was (and still is) an inspiration to many, doing incredible work to raise awareness about animal cruelty and acting as ambassador or patron to lots of charities.

I was feeling quite weak now, the cold having really kicked in, and my muscles, having been pummelled and pulled about so much, were painful. But you can always dig deep – and dig deep I would.

Kratu's movement is just spectacular to see. And once he was in his zone, I picked up the pace, so he'd automatically move into his extended flowing, floaty, pointy, paws and we sailed past a couple of the others. I was barely aware – all my focus was just on keeping the momentum, seizing this last chance to showcase him for the judges.

It was down to Kratu, as I was on my last legs now.

Once we had finished and the judges were deciding on their winner, I switched off completely; there was no way we would win. Not here. Not with so many outstanding dogs in the final. The winners of each class were beautiful, end of. Especially the puppy class, which had been won by such a cute, fluffy German Shepherd puppy that there was no way on *earth* that he wouldn't.

But what did I know?

Apparently, nothing. The reserve Best in Show went to a beautiful Bernese Mountain Dog. Then it was time to announce Best in Show. Peter Egan turned around then, but his gaze wasn't directed towards the GSD puppy. Inexplicably, he seemed to be looking straight at *us*. Then even more inexplicably, he said, 'Kratu!' I was stunned.

We were then called into the centre to receive a bin liner of yet more amazing goodies, including, for me, a clutch of Ted Baker treats. They were one of the main sponsors and I was delighted to see a beautiful pink handbag that I knew my daughter Scarlett would just love – I really wanted to give her something that would make her smile. I still struggled talking to her some of the time and this small gesture was one way of letting her know that I loved her. There was also a rosette the size of a dinner plate.

By the time Marc Abraham came and joined us to add his own congratulations, I was not far off fainting and virtually speechless. I really wanted to speak to both Marc and Peter, but I couldn't get the words out. My brain and mouth had disconnected and I was feeling as floaty as Kratu's paws when he moved around the ring.

But Cinder Tess still had that ball to attend! Back to reality, and back to Ergun, who had come to collect our three big sacks of prizes, and back we went, up to the car, both heavily laden, a tired dog apiece and near-exhausted ourselves. But my goodness, we were triumphant! As I looked at my enormous rosette, I thought, had that *really* just happened?

As Ergun's such a good driver, I had put him on my insurance, which meant once he'd manoeuvred us safely out of London, I could do a costume change on the way. Off went the fake fur gilet and yellow jumper I'd worn for the show and on went my favourite boho top, with its spangly, jingly, sparkly decorations hanging off the neckline. I always liked to jingle when I walked and tonight it seemed absolutely perfect – I was more than ready for that glass of champagne now.

The journey to Surrey took just over an hour. A long way after the kind of full-on day we'd had already. But just the honour of being invited was so special to me that I probably would have travelled twice the distance if I'd had to, with or without Ergun. It really did mean that much.

I could hear music before we were even in the grounds of the university, the thud of the bassline keeping time with the thudding of my heart, as my anxiety began ratcheting up. What had I been thinking, choosing to do this? I was about to walk into a huge festival where I would know no one bar Michelle. Suppose I didn't find her? What then?

We were directed through the entrance, told where to go, waved past a couple of barriers and eventually found a space in the car park, the dogs slumbering in the back still, both oblivious. Ergun waved me off with a grin – 'Don't worry about me,' he said. 'Take as long as you want.'

To my great relief, I spotted the Natural Instinct gazebo straight away, noting the large chest freezer that was normally home to packs of dog food at all the shows had been repurposed to house bottles of expensive champagne. I was just thinking how well a glass of cold fizz would go down when one appeared in my hand, courtesy of Michelle herself.

'So, did you do well?' she asked, when I explained I'd come straight from Pup Aid.

I ran through the highlights of our day, including Kratu winning Best in Show. 'A long day, though,' I added, taking a welcome sip of champagne, which was ice-cold and delicious. 'Especially with Raffy.'

She looked shocked. '*Really?* The lovely Raffy?'

'Yes,' I admitted. 'Time to join the others with their empty purses, I think.'

The penny dropped and she laughed. '*Ah*,' she said, 'I see. Well, when you book it with the vets, don't forget to tell them to send us the bill, will you?'

I gaped at her. '*Really*?'

'Of course!' she said. 'We sponsor him, don't we?'

I was amazed. This was as good as winning earlier. No, *better*. I'd had no idea how I was going to raise the money for Raffy's castration and just like that, it was no longer going to be a problem. Which meant so much. It was the biggest and best gift of the whole day.

My couple of glasses of fizz having turned into four now, I decided it was time to get back to Ergun and head home. Michelle escorted me back out to the car park.

'You must be so proud of what you've achieved,' she said as we walked. 'And then to come all the way here too. Such a long drive! And your Kratu, he really is a *very* special dog. We're so delighted to have you all on board.'

I felt myself blush. I couldn't help it, I was so deeply touched. People just didn't speak to me in that way and my 'thank you' could not have been more heartfelt.

Michelle couldn't let us go without thanking Ergun and saying hello to the boys, of course, so they all came out to meet her and, eager to interact with someone after their long snooze in the car, as soon as she sat down to give them a cuddle, they both tried to climb on her lap.

Which felt kind of apt. And she was right: I *was* proud.

Wow, what a day!

I spent the next one in bed. What with the cold, the physical exertion, the champagne and all the excitement, I was so spent that after seeing Ergun off to catch his train back to London, I was barely able to move. Which of course meant we all had a lazy day.

Every bit of me ached for the next couple of days. Well, apart from my brain, which was now going into overdrive as I could feel a germ of an idea taking shape. Much as we enjoyed the shows now

– and I was genuinely beginning to – it was starting to feel as if we should do something more, maybe something for the community. In Kratu I'd been given such an incredible gift and it seemed only right that I should share it. Plus, he loved people; he'd shown me that time and time again. So, could he perhaps become a therapy dog? He enjoyed interacting with people so much that I knew he'd be brilliant at it.

After all, just spending time with him was therapeutic for people. I'd seen it so often. The way they smiled when he looked into their eyes, the way their faces lit up. I had never known a dog who could charm people the way he could. Or who loved being around people more.

I was decided. And tomorrow, I would start doing research. Because if Kratu had a calling in life, surely it was this.

CHAPTER 14

Unexpected Questions

In order to be accepted to do therapy work, a dog has to pass a formal assessment. So, thinking I'd put all my boys up for it at the same time (no therapy work for my haughty, wolfy Maia, though – as if!), I read up on what kind of things would be included.

The list was long, but it all made perfect sense. It included no jumping up, no pulling on the lead, no objection to being petted, no barking or growling, no snatching at offered treats and (fairly obviously) no licking. Dogs needed to walk nicely to heel and have impeccable manners, sitting quietly when asked to and not overreacting to any sudden noises or distractions.

The owner, similarly, had to demonstrate that they were in control and responsible; that their dog obeyed commands and accepted their authority; that they kept them clean and groomed, that they clipped their nails regularly and that in an emergency, or when they needed to withdraw, that they were capable of handling them in any situation.

I had no worries about any of these as I knew my dogs were lovely.

We'd worked very hard and their temperaments were perfect. They all loved people and it was a joy to see how wonderful they were around them. So I found myself in the unusual position of having three suitable dogs. And, my goodness, they all passed with flying colours. Which was great. But then ... Well, not a lot.

I wasn't sure what I expected, and perhaps I'd been naïve, but where I'd envisioned travelling around spreading happiness and joy, it soon became clear that it wasn't that simple. Though Pets as Therapy were supportive and sent several emails about prospective volunteering opportunities, the kind of support I'd imagined might be offered didn't materialise – you were expected to organise everything on your own.

Which should have been simple, but where were my Prussian general genes when I needed them? In this case absent without leave. Some things floored me. This did; for some reason I had a big mental block about taking the next step forward. Had I had someone to talk me through all the forms (the insurance form, the establishment registration form, the risk assessment form, etc., etc.) and maybe to accompany us to the first session, perhaps I'd have found it a bit easier. I also felt increasingly lost about the rules. They were all in place for good health and safety reasons, of course, but just the thought of how many regulations I'd need to keep in my head every time I visited somewhere made the prospect of going through with it too complicated for my brain to process.

I let it go, feeling let down. All those good intentions and nowhere to take them. Kratu, though, obviously had a nose for where to go, because in early summer, while at a dog show, he took matters into his own paws. Otherwise, we would never have got started.

It had been a good day. Kratu had won Best Crossbreed, and then Best in Show too, and we were by then wandering around the various stalls that were set up, on a meandering route back to my car. We were just passing a stall where a local care home was raffling a bottle of champagne when he tugged on the lead, dived under their table and refused to budge.

I apologised for his behaviour, which, naturally, the lady didn't mind at all, because that was how the Kratu effect worked. We then got talking and when she mentioned that they were looking for a therapy dog, I told her Kratu and I would love to visit.

The deed was done and they were delighted. As was I, because it was Kratu who had chosen it, drawing me over there and refusing to move until we'd spoken and they'd agreed he could visit. Which we did, the very next week.

Over the coming weeks we visited that local care home regularly and Kratu was soon a familiar presence in their sitting room. One elderly lady in particular really took to him. She loved to stroke him and as he sat by her side, she would tell me about her life. She talked mostly about the past, often going back to her childhood, but sometimes, amid the fog of dementia, she had moments of clarity about what was happening to her, and where she was, and she told me how much she hoped it wasn't true. What on earth can you say, faced with something like that? I was so glad I could let Kratu take over and give her some comfort. Whilst she stroked him and spoke with such sadness, his big eyes watched her intently.

Where Kratu loved it, Raffy didn't really take to therapy work. He loved the attention, and the people, and especially the old people, but had a fear of going in through the dementia home's front door. I thought I knew why too. He'd been castrated by now and had had a traumatic experience at the vets. I'd asked them to let me lead him out of the recovery room after his surgery, but for some reason they didn't; he was led back out to me with his cone on and was evidently scared, the nurse not knowing how gently he needed handling in unfamiliar situations; she had no idea of his needs. The cone was enough to contend with in itself and having to go through that doorway on top was too much for him. Such a little thing in theory, but it had upset him badly and certain types of door now made him anxious.

At first, I would take him round the back, where the patio doors would already be open, but this was supposed to be enjoyable for him and with the conflict the doors created, it didn't feel right to put him through it, so I retired him.

With no such anxieties, Paqo often came with me and Kratu. I found it helpful as it meant Kratu and he could alternate and take regular breaks, from what could often be quite intense work. And ultimately, not work for the long term. Visiting care homes, on the face of it so straightforward, had turned out to be anything but. In the case of that home it was the resident cat that had me on edge, understandably, every time we visited. They tried their best to keep it outside whenever they knew we were coming, but as everyone knows, cats are laws unto themselves, so I never felt entirely comfortable. Maia's early influence on Kratu, and her opinions about cats, might have affected him, and it made me very wary. We then tried another home but in this case it was the heating that did for us. It was always on high, which left Kratu and me wilting.

My belief was and still is that, in doing therapy work, the dog needs as much consideration as the people who are being visited and though we loved to see the joy on people's faces, it had to be joyful for the dogs as well and I was fast reaching the conclusion that perhaps volunteering in a different environment might be the way to go.

Training, meanwhile, carried on just as it ever had. Being at the centre of my dog family meant everything to me; seeing them grow and develop into happy, well-adjusted characters was *my* therapy.

We were still training with Wendy regularly, usually once a fortnight, at Wood Green's Godmanchester animal shelter. And, by now, she was one of Kratu's favourite people. Every time we approached the place he would start sniffing the air, signalling his excitement by making his 'kettle boiling' noise – the best way to describe his enthusiastic squealing, which would intensify to ear-splitting loudness in the car from the first moment he caught sight of Wendy.

Being a dog trainer, Wendy couldn't allow herself to reinforce such wanton noise, so she'd turn and walk away and I was only allowed to let him out of the car once he'd piped down again. Or, rather, explode out of the car in a cloud of excited grey-golden fur, shouting, in his doggy way, 'I love you, my teacher!', which would necessitate another bout of her having to ignore him and walking away, and I'd have to walk him back to the car, put him back inside and start again. This would, on some days, take one heck of a lot of time. But you cannot contain Kratu when he is full of love for his favourite people. He adores her to this day and not only shrieks when he's around her but also swirls and twirls like a great hairy ballerina. I let him now – I just tell her to catch the lead and let him go. 'Sorry, Wendy,' I would tell her, 'it's a love thing. And he's not going to stop loving you, ever.'

And he'd obviously charmed Wendy too. Because in the spring of 2016 she asked me an unexpected question: would Kratu and I like to be on Wood Green's Rescue Dog Agility team the following March? As in Rescue Dog Agility team at Crufts?

Crufts? I had never been and had never particularly wanted to, either, because it was all about pedigrees, which mine weren't. The closest we'd ever come was Scruffts, also run by Crufts, for crossbreeds, the semi-finals of which were held at a show called Discover Dogs, at which Raffy had competed the previous year.

This was different. Crufts was generally accepted to be the world's greatest dog show and to be asked to be part of it was an incredible honour. But Kratu wasn't a Wood Green rescue so how could Wendy invite me? We were allowed, she explained, because we did so much training there, a kind of unofficial member of the team. There was just the one sticking point: that word 'Agility'.

'I can't do Agility,' I said. 'I know nothing about it.'

'Don't worry,' she replied breezily. 'It's only to show people how rescue dogs can have fun with their owners. Doing activities to help them bond. It's not *serious*.'

Really? I thought. Not serious? She had clearly forgotten who she was talking to. I could no more *not* take it seriously than fly. And I had less than a year to prepare.

No time to waste, then. So, I leapt into action. And a post on Facebook about it soon after got results when my friend Penel Malby introduced me to a lovely lady, Cat Clark. Cat was an Agility competitor who rented a field for her equipment and very kindly offered to let me use it, free of charge. I was so touched – yet more evidence that there were some truly good people out there. And by some stroke of luck, I was finding them.

The field was on the way to Godmanchester and along the A14; a road notoriously troublesome, with frequent traffic jams. I was a little daunted the first time I went there, because Agility was so new to me, and I hadn't a clue how to approach training with all the equipment set up there – the various jumps, the A frame, the tunnels and walkways – but having a course to practise on was such a great opportunity, even if we were minus a teacher.

First though, I needed to do some research. I got in touch with

Emma Gray-Sinclair, another Agility competitor I'd known since my early twenties, and Tig Tervs, a dog trainer I'd first met at Do As I Do. Between them and Cat, I now had some helpful basic pointers and armed with plenty of treats and a soft toy called Sheep which Kratu loved, we were ready to begin.

Getting a dog over a jump isn't as easy as it looks because they first have to learn to go ahead of you. In essence, I had to 'send' him over the jump ahead of me. Hence the toy, which I'd fling across the jump for him to fetch. Though the first challenge was to get him in a position *to* jump and teaching the wait-in-front-of-the-jump bit was more than enough to be going on with.

It was a whole new ball game directing Kratu to work his way around a course, but as usual, he took to it with intelligence and enthusiasm. And a lot of interest in other things as well. The field mouse who lived under the tunnel, for example. The horses who lived in the next field. Kratu loved to observe, delighted in watching life happen, but despite the wealth of distractions around him, he got there. Within a matter of weeks, he could complete a whole course, helped by the regular feedback I got from Emma, Tig and Cat, so they could tell me where we were doing well and how we could improve. This might 'only' be rescue dogs having fun with their owners, but this was still the iconic Crufts, after all. And though I didn't give a monkey's about doing well at Crufts for its own sake, I did care about doing the very best I could and making Wendy and the Wood Green team proud of me – that part I took *very* seriously.

It was also time to take something else seriously. Or, rather, some*one*: myself.

Life is often a series of steps forward and back. Progress, then many steps backwards, then try again. This was always the story of my troubles with communication. I had periods of time when things seemed to work okay and then suddenly, maybe prompted by a family issue or a difficult interaction with a new friend, the old habits would rear their heads, reminding me that I wasn't good enough and never would be; that I was a deeply flawed human being. Then bulimia, another of my old adversaries, would kick in.

I'd had years of different advice about dealing with my various demons and got referrals to new mental health teams every time I had moved house, still trying to find out why I didn't fit in, why I struggled to read and understand people, why I kept having these regular, exhausting meltdowns. That none had ever amounted to anything was still a constant nagging question mark, though increasingly I had run out of motivation to keep looking for answers, preferring to accept the limitations of my life rather than keep on and on trying to find answers that never came.

But now I was in a state of inner conflict. My life had changed direction. I had my dogs to think about and care for and I was increasingly desperate to be well. So, resolute now, I simply made a choice: I could choose to waste my time and energy, stuck on old patterns of behaviour, or I could try taking a new path. One I could walk with my dogs alongside me and with Kratu, my shining star, leading the way.

Looking back, it was a no-brainer. I was devoted to my canine family so I wanted to give them the very best of me. And to do that, I must try one more time to make sense of the struggles that resurfaced from time to time. The question WHY? still burned in me deeply. I had to find out more about the triggers that could set me off and how I could overcome them. It was too time-consuming and frustrating to go ten steps back every time I managed to go fifteen forward. Most of all, I wanted to do more with Kratu and I needed to be well for that. I didn't have the time or capacity for this to continue the way it had.

So, in the summer of 2016 I asked for a referral to the local mental health team, with a determination to find answers I'd never felt so acutely. Why wasn't my light coming on? What was that missing link?

Of all the labels that I'd been given the one that upset me the most was that I had 'borderline personality disorder'. What are you supposed do with such a harsh assessment of who you are? And what could I do about it, to try and make my life easier to bear? I refused to take meds – I'd had a terrifying experience with antidepressants when I was younger – so what other treatments were left? Basically, none that I felt would fit me. If I wanted to get better, I was on my own.

Before Kratu came into my life, my 'treatment regime' had been simple. With the real world so often triggering my anxiety and the bulimia that had been a constant part of my life since my early teens, my prescription had been to keep the world increasingly at bay, choosing to be a virtual recluse rather than interact with reality.

I had become bulimic, I knew, because communication was so hard for me and emotions, particularly around my relationship with my mother and the illness of my father, were so hard for me to digest. I made myself sick precisely to get rid of those emotions; I had to hurl them away with a vomiting force, to be flushed away, out of my body and sight.

I had also long managed my anxiety using drugs; I used to describe it as being cocooned in cocaine – satisfyingly numbing and also the only way I could ever sleep with a man.

Having Maia, having chemo and leaving my life in London had been the first steps in nailing that cocaine coffin down for good, but since then, it being easier to hide from the world than to engage with it, I had become increasingly reclusive.

Kratu had blown all that out of the water. He had pulled me – *kept* pulling me – out of my self-imposed isolation; we were now regularly stepping back into the real world together and I desperately wanted to be well. Not just on the odd occasion, but all the time. I'd moved from Witchford to Newmarket for clear, logical reasons so I could better help my dogs to live the lives they deserved without conflict. Little did I realise that doing that for them would put me exactly where I needed to be in order to get help for myself.

But that's what happened. My referral came through; I was now under a new mental health team, headed by a new clinical psychologist, Dr Oliver Hockley, and when I described to him how Kratu was making such a difference to my life (something perhaps only possible because Kratu was allowed to be right there beside me in his consulting room), in answer, he asked me a question. Had it ever occurred to me, or been discussed by anyone else, that my 'borderline personality disorder' might, in fact, be autism?

I told him it had, but that I'd never taken any notice of it, let alone researched it, because my perception of what autism meant – my idea of what an autistic person might be like or act like – felt so at odds with how I had always seen myself. It wasn't just that, though. I had learned to mask how I was feeling from a very early age and so effectively that I hadn't appeared to be someone in as much pain and internal conflict as I was. I had, in short, done a wonderful cover-up job. Too wonderful for the truth to have been seen before.

That day, he didn't only tell me he thought I might be autistic. He took immediate action, something I had never seen before, speaking to the team at the adult autistic diagnostic service which, by sheer luck in the healthcare postcode lottery department, I lived in the right place to be sent to. Such luck. Such incredible, random

Left: The day Kratu arrived and our adventures together began. © *Author's Collection*

Right: Kratu with Raffy and Maia on a wet and windy countryside ramble. They all walk on the slightly wilder side…

© *Author's Collection*

Kratu and I had great fun at Pup Aid and made plenty of friends. Kratu winning Best in Show was so unexpected!

Above: Kratu's first encounter with the amazing Peter Egan, who, as head judge, presented his rosette.

© *Julia Claxton Photography*

Below: Another year, more rosettes… Here we are supporting Lucy's Law Campaign with our pink rosettes at Pup Aid.

© *Julia Claxton Photography*

Our appearances at Crufts have become somewhat legendary thanks to Kratu's inspired freestyling and lovable antics. *Above left*: Kratu and I with one of the Crufts Agility rosettes. *Above right*: That iconic moment where Kratu had a little too much fun in that tunnel! *Below*: In full flight; Kratu in all his grace and glory. © *Natasha Balletta*

It was such
an honour to
perform at
Autism's Got
Talent!

© *Karen Nicholson,*
Little Pip Photography

Together we have achieved some amazing things, from attending a university lecture for animal psychology students in Romania (*above left* © Nicole Frobusch), visiting the house of commons, who needed a new speaker... (*above right* © Donna McDonald, Founder of *www.netmutts.com*) and attending the European Parliament with Maria Slough and Peter Egan. (*below* © Maria Slough).

Above: My daughter's wedding was a very special day for all the family – including Kratu and Polo! © *Griffin Photography*

Below: Time for tea?! They do love posing. © *Cassidy Meyer Digital Photography*

Left: Kratu and I, always together, always messing around.

© *Wolfhound Photography*

Right: Kratu winning the Social Media Superstar award. A dream come true!

© *Karen Nicholson, Little Pip Photography*

Kratu has changed my
life for the better, he is
my everything.

© Penel Malby Photography

good luck; they were considered one of the best teams nationally, as well.

Dr Hockley was clear, though: this wouldn't be a fast process. 'Be patient,' he said. 'There is a very long waiting list. Your referral could take up to a year to come through.'

Since I'd by now spent fifty-four years not knowing, I told him I thought I could probably wait another year.

But I was wrong. I couldn't help myself – I think I drove them nuts as well. Wanting facts. Wanting figures. Wanting timelines and constant updates. Which, on reflection, was a very autistic thing to do.

Perhaps it was knowing that that made their patience so exemplary.

CHAPTER 15

Kicking Down the Door

I don't know if it was my constant questioning, but my referral to the Bury St Edmunds diagnostic team came through much earlier than had been predicted, towards the end of December 2016.

The appointment, which was on 6 January, came and went in a blur. I remember emailing them to say I would be bringing my assistance dog, but very little of the substance of the meeting itself, other than that I was in a room in a hospital with two strangers, that the room felt very closed in, and that the air was stagnant and the lights much too bright. I have a fear of being locked in when faced with rooms like that and all I could think was *I want to escape*. It was only Kratu, lying calmly at my feet, that kept me there.

There is a lot of form filling in establishing a diagnosis of autism and the initial assessment also included a lengthy questionnaire, which I was instructed to take home, fill in and return to them. It was daunting in the extreme. And not just daunting – it seemed to have absolutely nothing to do with how or who I was.

Did I rock? No, of course not! Did I hum? Didn't most people? What was odd about that? On and on it went – was I considered too loud? Had I special routines of my own? Was I impulsive? Did I get distressed if my routine changed? (Oh, poor Celia, I think you could have answered that one for me!) Did I have food fads? (What a question! I wasn't a child!) Did I repeat words I'd heard? Did I smell things? Did I copy sounds? Did I ever sound rude and offensive without meaning to? (How would I know?) Had I ever been fascinated by one particular object? (Yes, of course! Kratu. My pony Caspar. The Q'ero teachings. Was that *abnormal*?)

Having got through the initial meeting feeling reasonably positive, even if scared, I began to look at the form in front of me with mounting horror. This was ridiculous. Upsetting too. How could I be diagnosed if the things on the form did not apply to me? Seriously agitated now, I reached for my phone.

I'd met Karen Nicholson a couple of summers back when Raffy was nominated for an Animal Hero award. Nothing had come of the nomination, but we'd struck up a friendship and she'd told me that she worked with autistic children. She'd also told me, more recently, that if I needed any help during the assessment, I should call.

I needed help. Badly. I called her.

We had several long conversations, over a period of days, and with Karen's patience, and her ability to help me see myself through fresh eyes, I began seeing the form differently as well. 'I don't do that,' I'd tell her firmly. 'Tess,' she'd argue gently, 'actually, you know, you've already told me you do ...'

It was an eye-opening process. Not just to see yourself through someone else's eyes, but also because, as we went through each item on the endless list, I came to realise that I must have buried aspects of myself so deeply that they had become completely out of reach to me. That I simply couldn't see.

It took me a long time to process what I was seeing, hearing, reading, but once I had, memories began flooding back. Each one, once acknowledged, was bright with new meaning. Of course I rocked; in times of great distress I had always rocked backwards and forwards. How had I not seen that? The only way I could rationalise it to myself was that it had been little Tess who'd rocked through those dark, traumatic moments, not me. I think I'd disassociated from her *that* much.

I had always hummed too. And yes, sometimes people had told me I was loud. And I had always had strange compulsions around food. I remembered living in Iquitos, in the Amazonian jungle, and every day I would eat and drink the same things, precisely: patarashca, a fish cooked in a banana leaf, and fresh coconut water. Plus, vast quantities of fresh, pure cocaine, straight from a jungle kitchen. Day in, day out, for weeks on end, never changing. It only stopped when I got on a plane and left for a new place, the fixation then completely forgotten.

I favoured foods of certain smells and colours. Colours particularly. I would eat something in a restaurant and would practise and practise so I could recreate it precisely at home. It had to be perfect, that was key – I had to make it exactly as it should be.

I liked sounds too. I responded to some sounds almost viscerally. Did I repeat words? I'd thought no, but now I saw I did. Only the day before my satnav had said, 'Turn left to Watford.' But it had sounded like 'waff-ord' and that had pleased me. So I drove along, saying 'waff-ord' to myself, over and over. For no other reason than doing so pleased me.

Once I found out what the words meant I realised how much

I liked alliteration (words starting with the same letters) and assonance (words with the same vowel sounds). Strings of words that sounded pleasing together. In private I would rarely call my dogs just by their names, it was always waccy paccy pack quack, Count Pacula, Don Paqolucci. Goosey honking Raffy gander, Raffy rooster. Kraty Waty Wooster. Kraty woo woo.

I would copy birdsong. And now dog noises too. Plus, my usual repertoire of strange noises – ones I found pleasurable to articulate. Noises which Kratu always responded to and would even, sometimes, try to copy himself. That was a good revelation – had I got something right, then? More food for thought; I'm sure a professional would say no, that's not possible, but I really didn't (and still don't) care – I knew the depth of our connection, our amazing communication.

I liked to touch things with certain textures. Peach skins. Fuzzy-Felt. Suede. A particularly smooth and shiny piece of my hair, close to the root. I'd touch the same spot on Kratu; our hair was so uncannily similar. Running my fingers over that silky spot helped me to relax. I remembered how I'd run my tongue over a peach skin, a suede coat. I had always loved the feel of stones, collecting them as a child. I even ended up working with stones in the Andes, where the Q'ero people believe they hold great wisdom.

And yes, I *was* impulsive. Often dangerously impulsive. It was one of the reasons I had been misdiagnosed with a personality disorder. I had thought nothing of going up the Amazon in a canoe at 4am in search of beer – a four-hour journey in a boat overloaded with people going to market, the rim only an inch or so above the waterline. This was the kind of river people fell into and sometimes never came out of, and though I recalled noticing this and thinking it slightly concerning that there might be crocodiles about, it was only afterwards, once we'd disembarked on to the riverbank, long after dawn, that the thought of piranhas even crossed my mind.

The further I got down the form, the more my life was coming into focus. What had previously been a collection of unrelated events and sensations – most now blurry – was beginning to coalesce and take solid form as the individual pieces of my life were slotting into their places in the bigger whole.

I can never thank Karen enough for her extreme kindness and endless patience. I'm quite vocal when displeased and filling in those forms sent me off the deep end several times and prompted the re-emergence of frightening flashbacks on a nightly basis. But, bit by bit, with her time and her help, I got through it. And I realised that perhaps I could have recognised those traits in myself years earlier, if I hadn't been too busy surviving in my dark, undiagnosed world. Or had taken that next, crucial step further towards diagnosis. But I think I had slammed a door shut in my head; it had been so touch-and-go whether I'd wanted to live or not that any more overload of information would have taken me down.

So, instead, I had become the queen of masking, and had thrown such a good mask over myself, over who I *was*, that I had all but made my autism invisible. To others, but especially to myself.

I'd learned to mask, in the first place, primarily to survive. I had been lost for so long, but after stopping heroin – showing an inner strength that still astounds me to this day – I made a decision: to learn to thrive in the dark world I now inhabited.

I had this strange ability to copy others. When at the bottom, in the darkness of my drug-using days, I encountered many different types of criminal and I copied some of the traits of the most successful – hardness, utter coldness, ruthlessness. I had clawed my way out of a hell pit into a murky dark underworld and found it was a place I felt comfortable in. I looked and acted the part. I *became* the part I played.

Mostly though, I masked to interact with men. That was the bottom line, the tragic truth of it. I couldn't bear to be touched, so in order to sleep with someone, I masked. It buried the pain and soon became my armour – second nature, born of necessity, to survive. Survival, for me, was also to observe other women. Women who looked confident, relaxed, in control. I copied them. Scanned every movement, every expression, until I looked the same, leaving the inner turmoil, the pain and despair, to come out only when I was alone.

That innate ability helped me climb out of hell. I could have stayed stuck in some pretty bad places. I could have stayed in violent relationships, could have carried on being used and abused. But instead I looked at people who had control over their lives. They might not have been your average role models but the successful ones in the murky underworld I had lived in were the ones I copied. I rose up and I grew in strength and ability. I wanted to be like the ones who had power. Not the ones people walked over.

I don't know what prompted it. Something deep within? My higher self? But one day, I felt a powerful and desperate compulsion to leave that world. To seek happiness, a better life. There had to be more. And that day, knowing I was done with it for good, I walked away.

Maybe I had got into it in the first place because of the way I was. But the way I was – the way I *am* – was also my strength to get out of it. I could see that now. It was at last making sense. And now Kratu had led me back to that same door and sat waiting patiently for me to open it. I looked at the door. I knew it so well. And now I was going to kick it wide open. No more locked door!

Looking back over my life with this new understanding was

as profound an awakening as any I'd ever known. It had been colourful and chaotic, sometimes exhilarating, sometimes crazy, often dangerous and always extreme. There is a Hunter S. Thompson quote that always seemed to fit me:

Life should not be a journey to the grave with the intention of arriving safely in a pretty and well preserved body, but rather to skid in broadside in a cloud of smoke, thoroughly used up, totally worn out, and loudly proclaiming 'Wow! What a Ride!'

That *was* me and I could not regret being me. And however hellish the lows, some of the highs had been ecstatic. But there was no escaping the reality that my ride had been so rocky in places that had something major not changed for me, my journey to the grave would have been a very short one.

I still wanted the ride, but now I wanted adventure rather than danger, thrills rather than risks, to still live a life that was true to my eccentricities, but always with Kratu's happiness and safety my priority. He had brought stability, calm and thoughtfulness to my life and I had finally accepted that when hurtling through it the way I did, it was okay to be wearing a seat belt.

CHAPTER 16

Enter Ducky

Filling in the assessment forms was only the first part of the lengthy process of finding out what made me tick. Now they had to be analysed and discussed by the multi-disciplinary team at the adult diagnostic centre. They would then decide whether I should go forward to a more formal assessment.

Which meant I had to wait again. To try to 'put it out of my mind'. A skill I simply don't have, because my mind is relentless. I hate waiting at the best of times and this was the worst kind of waiting, the anxiety eating away at my already fragile sanity and the words 'what if?' constantly rebounding around my head: 'What if you are not? What if they are wrong? What if this has all been a mistake? What if you've put yourself through all of this for nothing?'

What then?

It was fortunate, therefore, that just at the point when I was wondering exactly how I was going to get through the days and weeks and months without losing the plot (I'd already been warned it might be months before we moved on to the next stage) that Wendy reminded me that Crufts was coming up – in March 2017 – so I needed to start practising in earnest.

I was starting to have serious doubts now. I didn't want to look a complete idiot. I don't know why I hadn't done it before, but I now went on YouTube and looked up Crufts Rescue Dog Agility and promptly had a panic attack. I even shook. Then, practical as ever, I decided to add 'sounds of Crufts' to our training regime and as we practised the course, I'd have my phone balanced on a piece of equipment, blaring out Crufts audience noises at maximum volume.

I didn't expect miracles – I just wanted Kratu to do a reasonable course. I knew he could as we had all those videos to prove it. However, in Agility training, he was having fun and when Kratu was having fun, he would sometimes improvise and want to do his own thing, which meant keeping him on track was sometimes very hard work. Ducky, too (Sheep was no more, Ducky was his new favourite toy) suffered from Kratu's impromptu 'improvisations'; one day in training I couldn't find him until I heard 'squeak squeak!' coming from inside the tunnel and found him inside, having nicked Ducky, whom he was busy destuffing with great gusto.

So, this was perhaps going to be on a wing and a prayer. (And by 'wing' I mean literally as he already had a penchant for jumping the wings rather than the jumps.)

Most important was that I didn't want to look as if I didn't take it seriously. I had too much respect for those who did 'proper' Agility. It's extremely hard work and it had by no means been easy to get as far as we had.

The closer it came, the more terrified I became, though. I knew Crufts would be crowded, noisy and incredibly overwhelming and the only way I could banish anxious, negative thoughts was to tell myself that I didn't have to go if I didn't want to. (Which was never going to happen, but I'm very good at fooling myself ...) But although it was terrifying, deep down, I knew I would go. After the effort he'd put into his learning, I owed Kratu that – I could only hope we were on the same page.

Crufts, a four-day event held at Birmingham's National Exhibition Centre, is the biggest dog show in the world so people from all over the world flock to it in their tens of thousands. A shifting sea of humanity that is driven to come together, pulled in by the same strong canine connection.

If you've never been to Crufts, it's hard to really appreciate the scale of it. Multiple halls, multiple show rings, multiple arenas and display areas, and hundreds and hundreds of retail stalls. Think of the wackiest, most out-there, most unlikely dog accessory imaginable and you can be pretty sure to find someone there selling it.

If shows like Pup Aid and DogFest are like giant-sized village fetes, then Crufts – obviously indoors – is like a mammoth doggy Expo. An event almost on the scale of the iconic Ideal Home Show, by far the UK's biggest national event.

No surprise, then, that if I'd had to go there on my own I wonder if I would have gone at all. Happily, Wendy drove us in her roomy Wood Green van and essentially escorted us (well, mostly me) through the throngs and throngs of people to the sanctuary of the Natural Instinct stand, where Michelle was a very welcome vision. Even so, this was by far the scariest show I had ever attended. And I wasn't just floating around a show ring with Kratu, I was taking him round *an Agility course*.

We were so well rehearsed by now that I should have been

operating almost on autopilot; we'd certainly put in as many hours as a trainee pilot must. But in this case, it would be an autopilot without a human backup as my mind had gone AWOL.

I can remember hearing them announce him, the words 'Baron Kratu von Bearbum' bouncing around my empty brain. Then 'Raffy or Kratu with Tessa from Wood Green' and commentator Peter Purves (of BBC One's *Blue Peter* fame) saying, 'I am not sure what he is, a number of crosses, I would think.'

And so we began. Well, in theory. Kratu was much too interested in the divine dog odours and was having a good sniff rather than focusing on me. We did a couple of jumps, avoided the weave poles, then he headed off, in and out of the tunnel. He was totally immersed in having a good time, exploring the arena, doing a few obstacles and, as Peter Purves then noted, was indeed going wherever he wanted.

Kratu then saw me approaching to get him back on track and sped off to have some more time investigating. 'These dogs are not particularly well trained at Agility,' observed Peter. 'But it doesn't matter. They are having fun. Dogs do all sorts of things to have fun. And this one is having a grand old time.'

Wasn't he just! I managed to catch up with him and he actually listened, *finally*, and I was able to get him back doing the course. 'Biddable, but not all the time,' said Peter. Too right! Kratu then finished off with some spectacular jumps, almost hovering over them with his paws neatly tucked.

I was just relieved we had actually been out there. In the spotlight, watched by millions (I shuddered at the thought) and had done well, which in my book we had, even if not by Agility standards. At that point I didn't care if it was good or bad – I just wanted to get out of there, and into Wendy's van and get home. I barely remember being there – looking at the footage, it's like watching someone else. What I do remember is just how remarkable Kratu was in taking care of me. Because it was he who led me back, following Wendy through the almost molten crowds of people, through the arena, through the multitude of passageways and car parks, at every point calm, a constant reassuring presence, gently bringing me back from wherever it was I'd gone to.

It took me days to 'come back' from my first Crufts experience and during that time my main feeling was one of regret. Despite what Wendy had said about it being mostly for fun, I wanted more – I had wanted Kratu to do it well. But once I was back thinking clearly, I did feel I'd accomplished something. Just in the amount of fear I had overcome, the intrusive thoughts I had quashed, the way I'd managed among such an enormous number of people.

I had also seen how much Kratu loved being out there, doing his thing, and I realised I had a lot to thank Wendy and Wood Green for. They had pushed me towards an area I would never have thought of going to, had given me a whole new set of skills that I'd never contemplated learning and, best of all, had spent time exploring yet more of Kratu's talents. It didn't matter that he'd done things in his own way. I knew what he *could* do, when he really set his mind to it. It had also given me yet more food for thought. I liked doing things with Kratu. He gave me a confidence I hadn't known before and supported me through my anxiety. Most of all, though, was that he had fun. And if he could have fun, I reasoned, then maybe, just maybe, I could learn how to have fun as well.

Despite my anxiety about what might be to come with my mental health assessment, I remember that spring and summer of 2017 as a mostly calm and happy period. Kratu and I were by now doing regular therapy sessions at Kettlefields, my local primary school, which we loved.

I'd met the headmistress, Alicia Gadsby, at a local dog show and we'd discussed him becoming a therapy dog. Shortly after that, she'd become headmistress at Kettlefields and as the wellbeing of her pupils and staff was a priority, she invited Kratu and me into the school.

The first visit went so well, we soon became regulars, Alicia telling me that he had a real gift for making people happy and that he was the softest, gentlest dog she'd ever met. The children took to him straight away and he loved going to visit them (and Alicia too; when he arrived, he would bound straight up to her in her office and try to sit on her lap!). He broke the ice with the children with his repertoire of tricks. They especially liked 'bang dead', which I'd taught him in the beginning, and would roll around laughing every time.

It was a perfect fit: Alicia told me that he'd taught the pupils to 'be kind like Kratu', to consider others and help cheer them up if they were sad. You couldn't have found a better role model for children.

Kratu continued to amaze me with the size of his growing vocabulary, which meant we could add ever more new tricks and behaviours to our repertoire. The word 'kiss' for example. He knew the word kiss and that when I smacked my lips together and made a kissing noise, he'd get a reward for responding by touching his nose and mouth to my mouth. Sometimes now, he'd even instigate kisses on his own. He'd be sitting near me, watching me, and would get up randomly, then come across and do a little nose touch on my cheek or mouth – his own spontaneous kiss. I truly believed he understood it was a sign of affection and wanted to share it with me too.

I also taught him 'eyebrow wiggle'. He'd watch me move my eyebrows up and down – wiggle wiggle – and he'd then bark on cue and get rewarded. Naturally, I would laugh and that would be a treat for him too.

Oh, how those little things made me happy.

His big theatricals were pretty impressive too. We were at a show one day, having travelled there in my new car – a Skoda Yeti, which a dear friend from the show world had agreed to lend me the money to buy, after my old car had given up the ghost. (And then refused to accept repayment – an act of friendship that simply blew me away.)

I'd left Kratu and Maia in the back while I went to help someone handle a dog in the ring – with some water and the windows wide open. I returned to see two faces looking out miserably from what I could see were now completely closed windows. *What on earth?* I tried to open the door and they were, inexplicably, all locked, despite my having left them all open, with my keys and bag on the floor beneath the driver's seat.

How on earth had that happened? It didn't take much to work it out. Someone – a canine someone – had climbed under the dog guard, into the front of the car and stood on the central console where the universal lock button was located, presumably on his stealth mission to steal treats.

I found an ex-policeman who offered to smash the window; we would have little choice soon as it was already getting warm. He went to fetch a hammer, but when he returned with it, I asked him to wait – already tearful at the thought of smashing up my brand new car. (I'd already had a stone hit the windscreen and crack it on the way.)

While the dogs were obviously much more important than the car, surely we could fix this without resorting to using hammers? I went to the front and gazed at Kratu through the windscreen. I must give it at least one go, getting him to do what I wanted – which was to stand on that bloody lock button again! Meanwhile, the dog in question was once more sitting demurely in the back. Cue one of our classic Tess and Kratu conversations ...

Come here, Kratu.

No, Mum. Dogs aren't allowed in the front. You know that. I'm a good boy, I stay in the back now.

I began to do a little dance for him, calling him all the names: *Kraty waty! My little woo woo! Mummy's little boo boo!* And so on.

Nothing. Not a thing.

I tried again. This time I mimicked tapping with my hands – *Paw paw, Kratu! Touch!* – and finally, he eased under the dog guard and ventured forward. I then moved to the side of the car and began making tapping motions repeatedly. He is, after all, trained to touch objects with his paw and if he copied me, we were in business. And he copied me. *Smack!* went his paw on the stupidly placed lock button. (Not forgetting the stupid person who had left her keys in the car ...)

BOOM! Click went the doors. A small crowd had gathered for the tap-dancing show and everyone dived forward to open them. I have never been so relieved.

Better still, Kratu wasn't remotely fazed by his dilemma and went on to storm all his classes, even ending up with both Novelty Best in Show and Reserve Champion in Show. It was another example of our incredible communication as I don't think many dogs could have understood what was asked and done what he'd done.

They definitely need to rethink that lock though.

ENTER DUCKY

We were coming home with prizes all the time now to add to our growing collection. The wall in the dog room where I stuck up our rosettes was now a multicoloured mass of shiny, sparkly, beribboned frivolities, which fluttered merrily in the breeze when the back door was open and the hair bears went careering in and out of it. Laid end to end, these pretty ribbons might not have circled the earth, quite, but my bungalow, certainly. And then some.

And they kept coming. That June, Kratu repeated his success at Pup Aid by winning Best in Show at DogFest, and by early September, he'd passed both his Kennel Club silver and gold Good Citizen Awards.

The Kennel Club Good Citizen Award scheme promotes responsible dog ownership by teaching owners to train their dog for every life situation. There are four levels – puppy, bronze, silver and gold – the gold being the highest level of achievement, developing advanced skills between dog and handler. I felt such pride in him for achieving that – it felt like such a huge milestone. And a real sense of achievement myself.

I had also found friendship, of a kind I'd rarely known before. I'd found a true friend in Angie 'Chocolate' and another in dear, gentle Colin – it was no small matter that I now trusted him enough to give him a key so he could take the dogs out if I wasn't there, which he loved. He was still such a keen gardener, despite his advancing years, and I'd often be in his garden, picking the produce he always let me help myself to, and Kratu, who loved spending time in Colin's bounteous play zone, would scamper straight over to the bean canes and promptly cock his leg. Colin would always roar at him, but fruitlessly – he never stood a chance in hell of catching him.

'Pees and beans, Colin!' I'd giggle at him. 'That's what it is, pees and beans!'

It was a million miles from my former life, the years of crazy cocaine chaos – the all-night partying, the hedonism, the endless, endless masking and the increasing weight on my already tired soul. Once, I would go to bed only when the birds began their morning singalong; now I woke up with them, greeted the coming day with gratitude, loving not just the sound of the dawn chorus, but also the unique tones of Kratu's personal dawn chorus, when he'd wake me with his songs of the ancient Transylvanians.

I wasn't just in touch with nature, as I'd been when in the Andes. I now felt that I was *part* of it, in a profound and calming way: I was enjoying living in the moment. It was Kratu who brought me that stillness, that peace. That mental space in which to stop and smell the roses. It didn't matter that my 'roses' didn't smell much like roses. They smelled like Kratu. And to me it was the best smell in the world.

Another blue envelope arrived in late August. (They used blue ones so that people wouldn't avoid them, thinking they were bills. And they were right to. If they hadn't, I wouldn't have opened them.) And in September and October, I had two further meetings, a couple of weeks apart, this time with Dr Colm Magee and Dr Rhea Young. (They work in pairs because one might spot something the other misses, and so, afterwards, they can discuss and compare notes.) I felt out of my head at both appointments, almost trance-like, my brain resembling a marshmallow pillow of cotton wool. A defence mechanism, probably, because though the detail still eludes me, what I do recall was the sense of profound rawness. Because to have to discuss the truth in such detail felt as if someone had taken a Brillo pad to me, scrubbed away at the veneer protecting me for so long and exposed the very core of my true self.

I'd taken a decision to be brutally honest with the doctors – I knew it was the only way to move forward. That decision also meant telling someone the truth about my past for the first time in my life. It was very painful to reflect on rape and abuse (it would be for anyone), but at that moment I knew I had to share it.

It was very, very tiring and I was way out of my depth. I'd come so far already, but now the end was in sight, my feet twitched and my knees were screaming out to move. I wanted to run. Only Kratu's steadfast presence by my side kept me anchored in that consulting room. After all, this thing, this presumed autism, could be key to my whole life. We'd come this far, which was promising, but what if they said no now? Having exposed my trauma, I think I would have crashed at such a violent speed that I might never have got back up again.

It really was that important, because if it *was* true, then the horrible things that had happened to me would not have been my fault. But if it wasn't … It was something I could hardly bear to think about. That was a very dangerous point for me. Because the alternative meant they *were* my fault; that I was vastly flawed, fucked up, and had asked for all of it. That was almost too unbearable to contemplate. If I'd had to, I'm not sure I'd still be here.

So when another blue envelope arrived, just three days later, I sank to my hands and knees on the floor, unable to open it, my head buried and held in my hands. I heard a noise then, sensed something move and looked through my fingers. Kratu was sitting directly in front of me with his head buried under a blanket, copying me but with one eye peeping out so he could watch me.

I do as you do, he seemed to say. *You hide your head. Kraty hides his head. Am I a good boy?*

The intensity of his gaze burned into me through the dark and brought the light.

Yes, Kratu, I told him. *You are a good boy.*

I could do this.

I picked up the envelope and opened it with shaking fingers. But the words that swam before me were the ones I needed to hear. It was official: I had an autism spectrum disorder.

The relief was incredible. It washed over me in waves. I had to sit down because my legs wobbled beneath me. And no wonder because it was the single most important discovery of my life. I began re-evaluating everything that had happened to me and the more I read and understood, the more the weight began lifting as my past came into focus yet again and through this new and different lens. As everything I'd struggled with, from early childhood to the here and now, finally began to add up. It was as if I'd been drowning; submerged in dark, murky waters and now those waters were beginning to clear. I was surfacing; I was learning how to swim.

The journey was not without pain though. Knowing what I knew now was a release in many ways, but when it came to my children, it broke my heart a second time as I realised why I'd struggled so much as a mother. I'd just not had it in me to give them the things they needed and deserved from me. How can you give someone else what they need when you cannot give it to yourself?

There is no treatment for autism. We must simply do our best to survive in a world that is 'neurotypical'. And although you can join groups for autistic adults, that was never going to be for me. What would work, I realised, was to let everything go. To keep doing what I was doing. Using the energy clearing tools I had learned from the Q'ero people in Peru: Toltec recapitulation tools, energetic reprogramming and reclaiming of power. Hawaiian ones of *ho'oponopono* and forgiveness. These things might not work for everyone. Everyone has their own belief system, after all. But that tie-cutting became a huge part of releasing old pain. I wouldn't revisit it. Ever. I didn't need to or want to.

It was the hugest letting go I had ever done; it was shedding the guilt that everything that had gone wrong in my life had been my fault. I had worn this heavy, battle-scarred mantle for a very long time. It was frayed, muddy, bloody and embedded deeply into my skin, from the burden of guilt, the lack of self-worth, the self-hatred. All things I would now send up in flames.

Shamanic fire ceremonies are common in a number of belief systems and provide a powerful means for transformation and rebirth. By placing our old belief structures on the fire and turning them over to the universe, we allow ourselves to heal deeply, in the soul.

I was so ready and so determined to do this. Release this heavy mantle, throw it into the fire, then to walk away, lighter and happier and with a smile on my face. Towards Kratu. And as I walked towards him, I could sense little Tess standing beside him, smiling with happiness too, her hands burrowed deeply into his fur.

CHAPTER 17

Paw Pressure and Performance

There was an unintended consequence of my autism diagnosis. It might have been coincidence or my unconscious mind working overtime (probably both), but I was becoming more and more frustrated by things I saw and heard around the rescue of Romanian Shepherds. And the key thing – the thought that put the whole thing into relief for me – was a single word: 'Misunderstood'.

There was a reason why some Romanian Shepherd rescues were failing, I realised – so many dogs, having been found homes, heading straight back to rescue, and others, even more distressingly, being put to sleep – and that reason was now clear to me. It was down to them being misunderstood as a breed: they were guarding/working dogs and didn't work in a home environment.

Being misunderstood was the story of my life. And what was needed was education. For people to take time and effort to learn about these breeds so they could give them more appropriate training and care. And what better way to do that – at least to set the ball rolling – than to introduce people to Kratu himself? To show the world (well, there was no sense in doing this by halves, was there?) just what could be achieved with early socialising, commitment and dedication to education, and being shown the respect and understanding they deserved.

And where better to do that than Romania itself? My original plan, hatched that second, was to take Kratu on a trip back to Cluj-Napoca, where I hoped to be able to have discussions with like-minded people, those who shared my belief that changes in animal welfare were needed, not least within the still-expanding and deeply flawed rescue system that kept failing the dogs they sent abroad.

I also wanted to find out if I could interest people in seeing what could be achieved as Kratu was the poster boy for doing things the right way. So maybe, just maybe, if I took him to Romania with me, people would sit up and take notice.

Sometimes I find it hard to work out what neurotypicals want, or how they perceive things, so I had no idea if the neurotypical world would be receptive to my grand plan. It could easily fall on deaf ears so I could only follow my own beliefs and instincts. But I believed in Kratu and my instinct was that if people actually met him, there was a good chance that they'd feel that belief too.

I began planning in earnest, posting my ideas on social media and inviting others to join me. If I could get some traction then I knew I might get media support too and the more I could get of that, the more good we could do. I also needed to have some kind of itinerary – there was no point travelling to Romania with Kratu without a clear agenda and purpose. So I compiled a wish list: I hoped to be able to get a meeting with the Mayor of Cluj-Napoca and I hoped to go and meet a man there who did therapy work with dogs. I also hoped to see another man, Ray Dorgelo, who worked with livestock guardian dogs (LGDs) and whom I'd come across during my breed research. I also wrote to the president of Romania, for good measure.

Perhaps unsurprisingly the president didn't reply and Celia quickly warned me off the mayor, who she advised me was not very dog-friendly. However, she was friends with a radio presenter and might be able to get me on the radio. Better still, the radio presenter knew someone at the university in Cluj-Napoca, who might be interested in talking to me too.

It turned out she was right. Professor Alina Rusu at the University of Babeş-Bolyai invited us to a lecture that she would centre on our human–animal bond and which she would deliver to her animal psychology students.

I now had a number of invitations. All I had to do next was put my plan into action. I felt a surge of adrenalin: the Prussian general genes were all firing up and good to go.

I was also getting fired up about Crufts and a good deal earlier than I had been the previous year. This was because one of the usual criteria to be on the team was doing the course at Discover Dogs first.

Discover Dogs is a big show at ExCeL London and generally accepted to be the precursor to Crufts; it would be only Kratu's second large arena performance. Little did I know at the time that he was a rogue in the making, so I pressed on with training, nose firmly to the grindstone, entirely failing to spot that while I was immersed in my planning that Kratu was planning too. I just didn't have a handle on his motivation.

For me, it was simple. It's really hard to perform in front of strangers but if it's something I can do, it's at least bearable. It was the element of the unknown that made it feel scary, so it made sense to practise and practise so things didn't go wrong on the day. I was beginning to get to grips with autistic me now too; this determination would surely work in my favour.

However, Kratu had his own take on preparation. When he was motivated, fuelled by the desire for fun above all, his ancestral blood and genes simply took over. This was freethinking of the Transylvanian ancestral kind at its finest. Who needs a human trying to run things when he clearly knows best? Which was an issue because, of course, I thought I did. I was exactly the same as him and equally immersed in him doing exactly what I said, i.e. this brilliant course of perfect Agility. Neither of us realised what the other had in mind. Great minds think alike – just with slightly different outcomes.

I had never been to ExCeL London before, only looked at it online, and I doubt it will be a surprise to any reader that it looked like being my idea of hell. Multiple stalls selling things I couldn't afford to buy, thousands of people, hundreds of dogs, bright fluorescent lights and constant noise. Not my cup of tea at all.

And so, on the day, it proved to be. It was just as I'd envisaged, only worse. And though I remember seeing Marc Abraham at some point and saying hello, other than that, all the other familiar faces that I would like to have said hello to were nowhere to be seen; the trip from the Natural Instinct stand to the show ring obviously must have happened, but apart from that one moment, I can remember little of it, my autistic mind having emptied my thoughts and disassociated me from my surroundings.

Thank goodness for Kratu. He was by now trained to ground me and I really needed grounding that day. At multiple times he performed a task called paw pressure, which he could do in various ways. Paw pressure involves him putting his paw on my foot and applying pressure, or wrapping his leg around mine in a hold. When he thinks I'm worried, he does it immediately – he knows when I need grounding. His firm hold on me and presence helps me stay present. It is very easy to float away, but he catches that and brings me back to myself. He has this curious way of looking at me as he holds my leg. An intense gaze, as if questioning where I am. Looking back into those deep pools of wisdom in his eyes, I can catch myself and find calm and focus again, returning to the present.

One thing I do remember was standing and watching the last of the professional Agility people doing their thing with their dogs. My heart was pounding now, thudding out a rhythm against my diaphragm. *Idiot* me. What on earth was I doing here? I couldn't do *that*. It was all *way* too complicated.

I also became aware of a different need. A familiar one when the nerves started jangling: wee time. So, leaving Wendy holding Kratu, I hurried off to the toilet. And as soon as I returned, back the urgent feeling came. Was this real or just imagined? *No*, I said, fighting it, you've just *been*! Then came Wendy's voice, effectively putting an end to my dithering: 'Come on, it's time to go on. Move up to the entrance and stand in order.'

Stomach flipping like a stack of pancakes, I did as she instructed. It was now or never. I positioned him in front of the first jump.

Come on, Kratu, I willed him silently. *Remember all our training.*

I had Ducky in my hand (well, to be honest, what little was left of him) and now we were here, I wasn't sure if that was a good or a bad thing. Lots of owners use toys that they've elevated to 'objects of great desire' to fire up their dogs before going into the ring – kind of getting them into 'the zone'. But there was always the risk that Kratu would grab his darling Ducky when he shouldn't. Still, when in doubt look at what people who know their stuff are doing and do that. So, we took Ducky in.

Kratu *did* seem to remember our training. But, unfortunately, only for two jumps. Because straight after the second one, he stuck his nose down on the ground, clearly set on his own plan for the course. And why wouldn't he? So many dogs had been in this arena and nosy boy was picking up some great whiffs! Then he ran off to the other side to check out the audience – hello, audience! – and came charging back to me, alive with joy.

This is fun, Mum!

But then he seemed to remember that we'd come here to do something. *Ah, yes, the course, of course!* He returned to the routine. He tried to steal Ducky as we came out of the weaving poles, so we had a quick tussle, but then he saw the tunnel, so we were once again on track, at least until we reached the second-to-last jump. Now he went fully rogue, spinning on his heels and flying over it, but *in the wrong direction*. Then he was off. Dodging me at all times and with great speed and dexterity, he proceeded to do the course, finally, and with grace and panache, the only trouble being that he was doing the whole thing in reverse order. I only managed to catch him when he was ready to be caught – after he'd finished this defiant freestyle performance – in what would, sadly, prove to be Ducky's final, and perhaps greatest, performance.

RIP Ducky. But what on earth was *that* all about?

'The audience loved it!' Wendy reassured me. 'Seriously, they *loved* it!'

But I was mortified. Back to more training in preparation for Crufts.

As the year drew to a close, I knew we had a lot more Agility work to do, but I was also beginning to appreciate something else: that training with Kratu made me happy. He made me happy all the time, of course, just by being himself, but when we were training, there was an extra layer of joy involved. And I think it was because being part of the process which was leading to his achievements was so good for me too, teaching me both self-discipline and self-confidence. And self-worth as well; I couldn't recall a time when I'd felt so light of heart. Yes, I still had my heavy energy days, remnants from the past that could sometimes catch up with me and bring me down. That was all part of the normal balance of my existence and I knew how to clear it. But the more we trained, the more I felt my *life's intention* changing, and in so doing, I was releasing old patterns of behaviour that no longer served me well, leaving me a whole lot lighter and much more full of flowing, happier energy, connecting me to the moment, and to a lighter and happier life. I now wanted to work with this new way of being and make my dogs' lives the best they could be.

There was also more wonderful news; in late November, Scarlett told me that she and her partner Jesse were expecting a baby. She was surprised when I told her that I'd already known; I'd seen her a couple of weeks earlier and felt a subtle change in her energy. I was so happy for her – I knew how much she wanted to be a mother. Despite, or perhaps because of, her own unconventional childhood, family was of such great importance to her.

Happy times, though, are often when we let our guard down and allow new opportunities to come in. Because I had absolutely no intention of rescuing another dog – what with another Crufts to train for, and a Romania trip to organise, I had more than enough on my plate already – I had only been keeping an eye on various dog rescue groups as part of my research for our trip, not to get involved in another rescue myself.

But then I saw a puppy who looked so similar to Kratu that although I definitely didn't want another dog myself, curiosity kept drawing me back. He was one of seven puppies that had been thrown out on to the streets with their mother. They were *still* on the street, but the woman from the rescue group was caring for the little family; she brought them food every day and after raising the necessary funds on Facebook, had been able to give them their first vaccinations.

By this time, I only liked to do rescue work with Celia, but I thought it wouldn't hurt to contact the woman and at least try to find out how she operated. She spoke good English and agreed to supply regular videos and photos so I could see what the puppy was like. After seeing them, I could tell that he had a lovely, happy nature and based on that, I agreed to foster him, with a view to finding him a home.

I sent a picture of the puppy to a woman I know called Wendy (another Wendy) and she came straight back to me, over the moon: 'If I could have drawn a picture of my perfect dog,' she told me, 'this would be it.'

'It's your lucky day, then,' I told her. 'He's yours.'

Which also meant that I didn't need to foster him myself. So perhaps I should foster one of the others instead? Now I was all geared up to do it, it made sense. Plus, every time I'd looked at videos of Wendy's puppy, my eyes had been drawn to another puppy. He had the palest blue eyes and every time I looked, they seemed to be looking back directly at me.

In some aspects of my life, I'm still impulsive but never when it comes to dogs and rescue. The stakes are too high for anything other than precise decision making, always based on reason and *not* emotion. I asked for more videos so I could understand this one better and though he was bullied by his siblings and seemed to always give in, I could see the spark of an intelligence in those incredible blue eyes. I also knew his quiet nature was essential if he was going to fit in in our house. And with those stunning eyes – like little chips of Arctic glacier – I knew I'd have no trouble finding him a forever home.

But first I needed to find the financial wherewithal to bring him to the UK and foster him, so I phoned my similarly handsome, blue-eyed, polo-playing friend, David. We'd been friends for so long now that I had no qualms about asking him; with his eyes being almost exactly the same colour as Polo's, I decided, using my own brand of logic, that he'd feel compelled to say yes. And he did. After some light persuasion and lots of friendly banter, he agreed to pay Polo's fare and his kindness meant the deal was sealed.

By the beginning of December, it was time to pick the brothers up. Wendy and I both drove separately to Dover, where we were each handed several kilograms of exhausted puppy. Frank was large, just as Kratu had been, while mine was already about the size of a small Labrador. I decided to call him Polo, short for Polaris. Polo because of polo-playing David's generosity and Polaris because it's the star you can find in the night sky by following the straight line upwards from Kratu. (It's also the name of a Romanian refuse collection company, so it seemed fitting on that level too.)

In a matter of days, however, it was evident that Polo would need some rehabilitation training. Luckily for him, though, he was immensely clever and that keen intelligence and good temperament held him in good stead. He worked very hard with me and within six weeks he was doing nearly the entire Kennel Club Gold Good Citizen Award exercises.

Polo's intelligence also meant that he'd need a lot of mental stimulation; he wasn't a dog who'd be happy on a sofa, spoilt with treats, and only taken out on walks with no training. He needed that input and someone who understood his needs.

Polo was also undeniably beautiful. Which I knew would only

complicate matters further. He could so easily end up being adopted for his looks and as the days passed, I grew increasingly anxious, worried that if I let him go, I would keep on feeling anxious about his future.

Needless to say, it wasn't long before I'd talked myself into the decision that little Polo would be safest staying with me.

I'm still sure Kratu had something to do with it.

CHAPTER 18

'How Did He *Do* That?'

Crufts number two, in March 2018, was, once again, at the NEC and this time, calmer (well, slightly calmer), I was able to take in a lot more as Wendy and I arrived and parked up.

As a visitor, you're not allowed to take your pet dog to Crufts. Mostly because there are some 27,000 dogs already there, taking part in the various displays and competitions and, by extension, to be seen pretty much everywhere you look, many primped to within an inch of their probable patience. A lot of dogs also means there needs to be a lot of doggy toilets. There were plenty inside, but on the walk in from the vast acreage of car parks to the hallowed halls beyond, it was a different story. But this was when most dogs, some having been driven for many hours and miles to get there, really needed a toilet break. Which was fair enough because calls of nature had to be answered. But to my disgust (and I hadn't really taken this in the first time I went there), there were piles of poop every which way I looked, both on and around all the walkways into the centre, from tiny pips to splats, to mountainous dollops, some still steaming.

It's hard to find words for the people who allow their dogs to do this. These are dog lovers, dog exhibitors, dog advocates, dog *people*. Yet even at the most prestigious dog show in the world, there are the 'too posh to pick up' and also the disgusting, downright lazy – people who cannot be bothered to clear up after their animals. It's utterly, utterly shameful.

We were four today. Me and Kratu, Wendy and Polo. Polo was still very young, but had been gifted a pass by Natural Instinct, who had declared him to be a Very Important Pooch for the day. I also knew it would be a wonderful learning opportunity for him; a feast of new sights, sounds and smells, plus new experiences to get his ever-enquiring mind into. It was a monumental training day; if you could survive this, you could pretty much cope with anything.

For Kratu, of course, this was familiar territory and he could barely contain his excitement. And not just because there were so many lovely people to make a fuss of him – this was the biggest buffet of enticing doggy scents anywhere.

Once we got inside the centre – no small journey – I handed Kratu to Wendy. She was our teacher, after all, and so very used to handling him. That left me with Polo, much smaller and easier to manage. Quite a *lot* easier to manage in this hall of magical scents. Even Wendy was having her work cut out with Kratu, who was determined to forge ahead through the hordes; she ended up having to loop his lead around his chest and turn it into an impromptu harness, such was his determination to follow his own nose and agenda.

My own agenda was simple: to try and get through the period before it was time for us to go on without succumbing to the sensory overload. And the assault on the senses was huge. An ocean of people, some in shoals, others meandering aimlessly, some forming impenetrable thickets around this stall or that stall, or dashing purposefully to this show or that imminent demonstration. Dogs underfoot everywhere – large and small, sleek or hairy – and a constant angry buzz of white noise.

What most of the regulars and professionals tend to do is meet up and network. I knew there would be a few people I'd already met there, but I knew better than to try and join in, because, as ever, when in autistic head-space mode, I would probably walk past my own daughter and not recognise her.

I'd taken Kratu's lead back by now – I could only bear to be parted from him for a few minutes – and I knew he was struggling a little too. In his case it was because to get from one carpeted area to another, we had to cross a sea of 'danger drains'. For some reason Kratu could hear the underfloor network of drains and could only get over them by pulling faces and adopting a peculiar funny walk. Maybe he was just copying me – it would not have surprised me if Wendy had told me I was doing a peculiar funny walk too (I could only hope I wasn't doing the funny faces as well). I made a mental note that I would have to ask her.

Whether true or not (I hoped not), by the time we'd arrived in the third hall – the one we needed – Kratu and I were glued together like two sardines in a giant can, him helping to steer a course for us through the multitudes of people to the sanctuary of the Natural Instinct stand. While Wendy went off to meet up with friends and colleagues, it would now be my safe haven before it was time for our performance. Kratu was pretty happy too, though his motivation for getting there had been rather different. It was a brilliant opportunity to go on a quick robbing spree, snaffling any treats he could get his paws on – and there were bowls of samples everywhere. And where Kratu led, little Polo naturally followed. Not to be outdone, he stole a load of tiny teddy toys.

I had an hour or so to wait and a couple of friends stopping by provided a welcome distraction, particularly my Romanian friend Dita and her husband Sorin, who breed pedigree Mioritic Shepherd dogs and who had helped me to research the different types of Romanian Shepherds. I found it amusing that a rescue dog native to their own country, a roughneck crossbreed, was right there on the stand at the world's largest pedigree show and keen to greet them. We also caught up with another Wendy, the one who had adopted Polo's brother, Frank. She offered to look after Polo while Kratu and I were doing our thing, which was a weight off my mind. And just as well because I was wilting under the current load, so much so that by the time the first Wendy came back to collect me for our session, I had regressed to the extent that it must have been like escorting a toddler – I recall almost nothing of the trip from the Natural Instinct stand to the main arena, only the strong, steadying presence of Kratu by my side as we mirrored each other in our 'Ministry of Silly Walks' walks.

The biggest arena, where we were to perform, is a bit like the Centre Court at Wimbledon and as we made our way down the long, carpeted corridor, I kept all my focus on the wiggly little stump of a tail in front of me – Kratu's antenna of happiness – because if a single thought strayed to the audience in the arena, fear would have stopped me in my tracks.

We 'performers' had our own special cordoned-off walkway in the middle, with members of the paying public walking either side, and I was aware of the oohs and aahs Kratu was attracting – as he does every single time, wherever he goes, because he struts his handsome hairy stuff so well.

It did little to quell my nerves, so I was glad when we got there and could head off into the privacy of the waiting area. There was time to take stock here and to practise if you wanted – there was a small area with a jump in it for the use of the serious Agility people. There was also a coffee machine (but I daren't – I'd only need a wee) and a melee of others, all doing just as we were, awaiting their moment in the spotlight.

The longer I waited, the more my confidence shrivelled; the little I'd come in with – already on the small side – had shrunk to the size of a pea. And the wait was long. We were one of the last pairs in the final round, the Agility displays being conducted in size order, from the smallest rescue dogs through to the largest. By the time our turn came, I'd not only forgotten who I was, I couldn't even fathom what my hands were for – even which one was left and which was right.

Then came the nod from Wendy: this was it, time to go.

We walked in, me keeping my gaze to the ground. If I got so much as a glimpse of the audience and the vastness of the arena, I thought I might melt into a little puddle on the floor. Somehow, I reached the spot where I was going to start the routine. Now to the task at hand, which was to put Kratu into a 'sit' in front of the first jump. I couldn't look at him because I knew he was staring up at me and if our eyes met, it would be a case of tears or giggles, neither of which would be helpful right now.

I touched his cheek and willed him to be good. Whether this moment of connection was to influence what happened in the next two minutes only he knows. I walked on my jelly legs to the other side of the first jump and looking back at him, I could almost read his thoughts. His eyes lit up and glinted, and I knew what they were saying to me: *I know this place, I like this place. There is fun to be had here.* He clicked into gear and popped over the first jump. Then it was time for a quick sniff, a smell that had his name on it.

The commentator, Peter Purves, clearly remembered him from the previous year ... Well, sort of. 'He's a crossbreed, or *she's* a crossbreed,' he added helpfully. 'Well done, Kratu, good start. We don't have to pay a *lot* of attention.'

Kratu evidently agreed because now he was off on a side-mission. Quick hello to the audience, more sniffing and snuffling. Then he saw me and realised he was supposed to do the jumps, so he popped over two more before seeing the ladies in pink at the edge of the arena and going over to say a quick hello to them as well – only to be rebuffed, one of them laughing as she raised a hand to stop him. They were stewards, there to do a job and not to stroke him!

Peter, now chuckling, had also stepped up a gear. 'He's a cross-breed of all sorts,' he mused, 'and hasn't a *clue* what he's doing!'

And from where I was standing, he was right. Kratu woofed and woofed again, asking for approval from the audience: *Look at me! Isn't this fun?* And off he went again. Busy lapping it all up, he swerved the next jump, only to spin around and fly over it backwards, at which point we were heading to the weaves – a component he could do very well.

Peter clearly had his own ideas. 'Now can we get him into the weave?' he wanted to know. 'I shouldn't think so for a second!'

And he was right. Kratu was having none of my distracting him with those things. He was too busy looking at the audience and feeling the energy.

Then came the first tunnel (and he does love a tunnel). In he flew so I ran to the other end of it to wait for him to emerge. But where was he? My mouth dropped open in astonishment, Peter Purves' too before he observed, 'Oh this is ... He's stuck ... OH, HEYYYYYYY! I love it!!! Hahaha – there's no room for him to turn round in there!'

But apparently there was; in that split second he'd done exactly that and come out of the same end he'd gone in. 'How did he *do* that?' Peter said. 'That was brilliant!'

As soon as Kratu saw me, he spun around again and dived back into the tunnel, emerging only to go sprinting off again, taking a jump with a great flourish, flying across to the A frame, charging up and over it, then down into the second tunnel before sailing over two more jumps at such a speed that he almost headed right out of the ring altogether, but for a quick handbrake turn, so, not quite done with this massive green playground, he could do one last jump.

'He couldn't care less, could he?' observed Peter.

The audience by now were roaring with laughter. They had fallen in love with my dog as much as he had them and the applause all around us was almost deafening. As for Kratu, his focus had by now returned to me and wiggling his little tail stump, he bounded straight over, where my arms, which now felt like soggy spaghetti, could encircle him.

My God, how I needed that contact, that moment! He was real. *This* was real. We'd done it. In our own way, admittedly, but we had achieved something huge here. Kratu had completed the course in his own way, true to his nature. And I had overcome my own hurdles and obstacles too. In that moment, we were both winners.

Peter Purves' last words really couldn't have been more apt: 'He is the reason Tessa gets up every day.'

I left that show ring with a profound sense of relief. I'd got through another Crufts and as opposed to last time, I'd been fully present – well, mostly – to take in more. Even better, though, we had done some Agility. No, we might not have done all the right things the right way in the right order, but we'd done it. And Kratu had loved every single minute he was out there and what could matter more than that? It was enough.

By the time my heart rate had returned to something approaching normal, the final pairs had done their routines and the Rescue Dog Agility display was done. There was no judging here, no winner or losers. Back in the waiting area, when it was time for the inevitable photos, I popped Kratu on the largest podium: the winner's one that, come Sunday, would be used for Best in Show. Well, for me, he already was, after all.

My whole focus now was on getting out and getting home again, so when we were back at the Natural Instinct stand and my friend, a dog trainer called Pat Wells, told me Kratu had 'gone viral', it took a few moments for me to take it in properly.

'Gone viral?' I queried.

She nodded and grinned. 'He's up to 8,000 views now.'

'Eight *thousand*?' I couldn't even process what she was telling me.

'Probably more by now,' she said. 'People *love* him.'

Which, of course, I knew. I had always known, but it would be a couple of days before I would realise just how much. My post on Facebook that evening said it all:

Wow. What a day ♥ *Proud of my boys. Kratu for an out-standing and wonderful performance. Polo for incredible calmness and beautiful manners for such a little rescue boy. And to see some special friends. Amazing day ... wow! Disbelief at the Kratu love around the world. I am so happy people can see what I saw all along. It wasn't my delusional mind ... He is full of love. He is full of joy. He does adore people. He does smile. He does make everyone laugh as he*

*is a natural performing clown. He is actually very clever,
kind and compassionate and the world smiles with him.* ♥
Wow ... Kratu. ♥ *I got something right finally. You ... My
darling boy.*

I went to bed that night with a big smile on my face, but no
idea that when I woke up the next morning, I would have a new
understanding of what 'going viral' really means.

CHAPTER 19

A Consummate Professional

In less than a month it was April, and we were going back to Romania.

I woke up long before my alarm, the sky dark and star-speckled and my stomach in the grip of the inevitable knots that had been gathering since before I'd gone to bed. It was stupid-o'clock (as it tends to be when you've booked bargain flights from Luton and you're taking a dog) and I needed food and strong coffee to get my cogs to start turning after the exhausting frenetic whirring of the previous night.

I headed into the kitchen, where the dogs looked up at me, sleepy and confused – as they would be, given it was the middle of the night. Except for Kratu, that is; he was instantly on his paws and ready for adventure, simmering away, almost shivering, in his excitement.

I managed not to wake Ergun, who had got the train up from London the evening before, the plan being that he'd look after all the other dogs for me, with the assistance of Colin next door. I had written out a list for them, with some million or so rules, most of which I knew would be broken. But it was one aspect of the trip about which, mercifully, I wouldn't worry – I had complete faith and trust in their care.

By the time I'd checked and double-checked all the paperwork – eTickets, hotel booking, necessary passports for both of us – the taxi was already idling outside. This was it, then. We were off on our trip back to the land of Kratu's birth and as he jumped into the footwell to snuggle down between my knees, even the thought of the stressful journey ahead couldn't dampen my sense of pride that I was actually doing this.

It had been a little under three weeks since we'd done our Agility at Crufts and I was still reeling at what had happened afterwards. The video they'd shared that day (*Krazy Kratu Kreates his own Kourse*) had, by the Sunday, attracted almost 2.5 million views. That had been mind-blowing in itself – I struggled to get my head around the numbers – but within ten or so days, it had risen to *8 million*. And it wasn't just the numbers that had blown me away, it was the messages, which had come thick and fast, right across social media, and from what looked like every corner of the globe.

And perhaps no wonder because the mainstream media had gone mad for him. 'Krazy Kratu', as Crufts had dubbed him, was everywhere suddenly. While I decompressed at home, with my usual post-stress cotton-wool cloud head, there were Kratu stories popping up everywhere. From the BBC and ITV, and almost all the national papers, his fame spread to what seemed like every corner of the globe, including major news shows in the US and Australia.

It was difficult to keep up; generally, the first I knew about this frenzy of coverage was when I'd go on Facebook each day and find hundreds of new notifications and all so joyful, so encouraging, so full of love and kind thoughts. Just trying to respond to them all was exhausting. But could there have been a better prelude to the trip I was about to take with my amazing boy? No, it was simply incredible.

Despite my call out the previous November, and the enthusiastic response to it, our party travelling to Cluj-Napoca was very small. Just me and Kratu, the lovely photographer Nicole Frobusch and a young couple I knew from Facebook who also had a crossbreed Shepherd, and who were keen to see his homeland as well. I wouldn't see any of them until we had boarded the plane, however: because I had Kratu as my assistance dog, I'd been asked to arrive earlier so we could be escorted through security and right out to the gate, where we'd apparently be among the first to board.

Luton Airport was quite a drive away and I was lucky with the driver. He loved both animals and healing – it turned out he was a big fan of reiki, the Japanese art of hands-on healing I practised – and wanted to know all about my energy work, so we chatted amiably for the entire journey, along the mostly silent, empty roads. The airport, on the other hand, was noisy and busy, every bit as formidable and daunting as I already knew it would be – a stress only magnified by the obvious complication that I was with Kratu, a big shoulder bag, and a badly behaved wheelie case and was thrumming with anxiety as I didn't know where to go.

Thankfully, all the ground staff were lovely, but right away it was obvious that Kratu didn't approve of the floor surface. He was tapping his paw on it, rolling his eyes and doing his John Cleese Ministry of Silly Walks walk, but as usual, he soon began to charm everyone around him, particularly the lady assigned to us, whom Kratu entranced on sight. Though my nerves were jangling like a bunch of wind chimes being hammered by a hurricane, she did a good job of keeping me as calm as could be managed, given that I was heading to unknown and potentially very scary territory. How would Kratu react to being taken up that glinting silver staircase and into that monstrous great machine?

But I needn't have worried. He was slightly cautious, but sheer determination got him up it and once on board, he settled down like the VIP he was, sitting so serenely next to me, with not even a flinch on take-off, and then dozing through almost the entirety of the flight, only waking to quench his thirst.

At the end of the flight he was happy to pose for a photo with the pilot, who came into the cabin specially to meet him. It was the first time he'd ever flown with a Very Important Pup, and a Romanian one too. Another first and we hadn't even got there!

As before, Celia had driven out to the airport to meet us – and was late. I was growing increasingly anxious again now, new fears crowding my brain. Would the hotel be okay? Would there be safe places to walk Kratu? Would I be able to find decent food for him? (Obviously, I couldn't travel with his raw food.) Would the arrangements I'd put so carefully in place *stay* there?

Clearly not. Having dropped Nicole Frobusch off at her place, Celia took me, Kratu and the two girls to the hotel I'd booked for us, but as soon as we got inside I knew I couldn't stay there. The girls were happy enough, but my and Kratu's room was right next to a door on a main corridor and I knew – because it happened – that it would bang every time anyone used it.

So, we trooped off to nearby Central Park and over coffee I did some googling with Celia, eventually finding a little family-run boutique hotel, who, when I called them, agreed that I could bring Kratu. Indeed, intrigued by his celebrity (I think they googled him themselves), they said they'd be honoured to have him as a guest.

Despite the complications, I knew I had made the right decision. The hotel was elegant and tastefully furnished and the staff could not have been more welcoming to Kratu. There was also a little dog park nearby so I could give him some exercise off the lead. I felt happier than I would walking the streets with him.

Then it was sushi with Celia and a very early night. And after metaphorically holding my breath since my alarm had buzzed at 4am, I could finally take stock. As I lay there listening to Kratu settling himself down beside me, I breathed a very long sigh of relief.

The following morning, we got down to business. With the two girls heading off to see the local sights, Celia and Nicole picked us up for a meeting with a man she knew called George Mosoia, who ran a therapy dog business from his home. It was all very professional and I could see he took his work very seriously – there were two impressive therapy rooms and everything was so clean that we had to wear blue plastic covers over our shoes, which put me in mind of my old Jimmy Poos and also ruined every single one of the photos!

George was a lovely man and one of the first people I'd come across working with therapy dogs in Romania. Kratu could see it too; he took a shine to him straight away and even sat on his lap in his favourite bearbum way.

George was also generous. Having pronounced my lead rather old and somewhat battered, he presented me with a new one, a space-age affair made of rubber. I was so touched by his kindness (and he was right, my 'old' faithful was exactly that) and left him feeling happy and optimistic. For all I'd read about and heard, and, indeed, had seen with my own eyes, there were clearly lots of people who were doing what they could to create change; he was one such person and it resonated with me greatly.

The following day, the two girls once again headed off to explore the city and Celia drove Nicole and me to Babeş-Bolyai University, to attend the lecture Alina Rusu was giving to her animal psychology class.

I had George's new lead with me and immediately wished I hadn't – I missed my old faithful, with its multiple knots. The heat in the lecture theatre was intense, to put it mildly, so I regretted my stupidity in thinking it would work – my sweaty hands meant George's lead kept sliding out of my grip and because it was made of rubber, I couldn't put any knots in it.

Still, Kratu was the consummate professional. I don't think I ever felt prouder of him than I did in that university lecture theatre, watching him engage with all the students and pose for endless selfies. It struck me that *I* hadn't taken *him* to Romania. Quite the contrary, it was him who had taken me. And he was absolutely where he loved to be: at the very epicentre of attention. Better still, I knew how much this kind of thing could make a difference. It seemed so obvious to me now that change, lasting change, requires an emphasis on education and the fostering of new attitudes in the next generation so to see him interact with all those bright young people was wonderful. They in turn seemed mesmerised by him, gathering round him with such respect and gentleness, and to watch all this love was a beautiful thing. Yet again, this was a different kind of Romania to the one I'd seen before, these young people so engaged and so interested and positive. They were seeing first hand what education and training could achieve, including the very fact that a dog known for guarding, and mostly kept at arm's length, was there with them, right in among them, connecting. It was an incredible exchange of energy and a vision of what *could* be.

We had also achieved the kind of publicity I had worked so hard to attract. Perhaps not so surprising as it was, for them, momentous: this was a Romanian dog, from a Roma camp, flying back into Romania. But not just any Romanian dog: this was the famous Kratu, who'd charmed the world with his antics at Crufts! So, the lecture was filmed by not one but two major TV stations and a reporter covered the story for a national newspaper too. I think they were proud that they could call him their own and by the end of the day, Kratu had once again made his mark and left a huge hairy paw print on their hearts.

There was also, for me at least, a standout moment. While we were filming in a nearby park, a small group of parents and children had gathered, their mouths gaping in what looked like astonishment. Alina Rusu had come along as well, so she could translate for me if needed, so I asked her to invite them all to come and meet Kratu and reassure them that he'd be happy for them to stroke him.

Which, of course, he was. Their delight was evident and they all posed with him for photos, but what struck me most was the reality that people were routinely so wary of dogs, and especially dogs who looked like Kratu. It really felt as if we'd done something of inestimable value in showing them that it didn't have to be that way.

The day after the lecture we went to meet Ray Dorgelo. Originally from the Netherlands, where he had worked as a dog trainer in the Dutch army, Ray and his wife had made Romania their home in 2016. Now a respected specialist working with Carpathian Shepherd dogs, he knew a lot about their history and character. He was also a great champion of the local human shepherds and had agreed that he'd take us to meet a local one, who had working livestock guardian dogs, and show us just how many different crosses there were working in Romania and a little about their different characteristics.

This took us deeper into the countryside of Transylvania. It was a very strange experience, as if we were peeling back civilisation layer upon layer to another time. Ray and his wife lived very simply there, no mod cons whatsoever, and this lifestyle was their normal. And it was clear that it suited them well. Yes, it was basic, but bucolic, with goats and chickens running in the yard and a small pack, half a dozen or so, of working Carpathians. (Which meant leaving Kratu in the car with Celia for a bit as they'd never accept a strange male in their midst.)

After a quick check on Kratu, Nicole, Ray and I walked up the hill to meet Ray's shepherd friend. The landscape, though beautiful, was bleak, dark and cold, and under the leaden skies, it felt as if we were heading even further back in time. The shepherd's hut, where he lived with his dogs, was even more primitive. No running water or electricity, just the bare wooden bones of a structure, with a wooden bed, covered by a couple of old sheepskins. The dogs here were fed and cared for, seemingly happy enough in their skins – none of them cowered in the way Tutty had when we'd first seen her. But even so, this was a hard life for them, with little in the way of comforts. One dog in particular caught my eye because he looked so like Kratu and I had a profound 'there but for the grace of God' moment. Because this could so easily have been his life as well, had mine and Tutty's paths not crossed when they did.

And I knew that not all shepherds were like this. Many dogs were beaten and cruelly treated – I had seen the evidence with my own eyes – but a lot of the country people could be very attached to their dogs too, caring for them as well as they could, just as generations before them.

There was no getting away from it, though: this was a poor, harsh existence. On our way back to the car, we walked past what looked like a dump – piles and piles of plastic rubbish and random junk, a human blot on the beautiful natural landscape.

'Please don't photograph that,' said Ray.

I hadn't intended to, but it hit home that he was fiercely loyal to his adopted homeland and didn't want yet more evidence of its failings put on social media. I reassured him that every country has the same rubbish pollution, but it was a thought-provoking, sobering moment.

It was so good, and so instructive, to meet and spend time with Ray. He was incredibly helpful and as committed to these types of dogs as I was, to the extent that he agreed to make the trip to the UK later in the year, so the staff at the Wood Green charity could learn more about livestock guardian dogs breeds (and the crosses that were going back into rescue at such an alarming rate) and how to manage them. And, hopefully, as a result, find better homes for them.

There was just one last mission that I was keen to accomplish. I don't know why, but I felt this powerful need to return to the Roma camp just outside Cluj-Napoca where Kratu and Raffy were born. Unfortunately, this did not go down well with Celia. She hates some of my ideas and hates the drive there as well. But Ray kindly agreed to follow us in his car, just to be sure of our safety.

We went on our final day and I was shocked to see how much everything had changed. The dirt track was no more. It had now become a proper road, and as we pulled up outside the military camp to see if we could spot any dogs, I could see further along to the Roma camp itself. The previously sprawling camp was now just a small huddle of huts and rubbish and the place where Tutty had given birth was no more.

We soon attracted the attention of a patrolling soldier.

'Oi!' he shouted. 'What are you doing? Move along!'

Ray went over to speak to him, explaining the reason we'd come, and the soldier told him that as far as he knew, only one of the dogs that had previously lived there was left. He was still keen that we move along and by this time a horse and cart had pulled up, its young driver screeching to a halt, a great grin on his face.

'You want to take my photo?' he asked us. The girls duly did and Ray and Celia both spoke to him. He was from the Roma camp, he told them, and he seemed keen to chat, so, mindful of the soldier – still keen that we go and park elsewhere – we got back into our cars and drove a little way down the road, by which time the young man on the cart had already raced ahead, in the way young men with wheels under them often seem to.

Celia explained who Kratu was and I got him out of the car so that he could say hello, by which time another couple of men had come out and joined us. Unlike the first man, they were suspicious and unsmiling, but when they heard the name 'Tutty' they all nodded in recognition.

'TUTTY SON!' one of the men said. 'Oh, TUTTY!!!!! Tutty is living the life now …' he gestured grandly, 'Tutty is on the *sofa* … Tutty is eating the *very* best food …'

It was all said with a great flourish, the man laughing as he spoke, and, despite the still menacing presence of the men standing behind him, I got the sense that, in fact, they *had* cared about Tutty. Perhaps letting her go hadn't been just about money. Maybe on some level they were pleased to know that she was seeing out her retirement in a better place.

I like to think so anyway. But who knows if that's true or not? Some might call it naïve. I still like to believe that was the case and I was glad to have that second glimpse into their world.

By this time I was picking up on the slightly strange vibe that Kratu, glued to my leg throughout, was clearly feeling: I could tell he wanted to go. So, we went. But I was pleased we'd gone. Pleased we'd had this meeting, this strange interaction. Four years earlier, Kratu had left this place as a raggle-taggle puppy and had now returned as a people's champion of Crufts, known around the world. And this would be goodbye; also closure. From that place had emerged a bright shiny diamond, but it was also the final act in Tutty's story, which had, of course, become my story too. Because in hearing her cry for help, and saving her, I had also saved myself.

As our flight back to the UK wasn't until late in the evening, I had managed to cram in one further meeting on our final day. Vlad Vancia was a young scientist with a passion for positive reward-based training, something of a rarity in Romania. As well as being an animal psychologist at the Romanian Society of Anthrozoology, he was also a writer and podcaster. Having read and heard so much about him, I was very keen to meet him.

I was not disappointed. He came to meet me and Kratu at our hotel and we discussed the negative dog training methods still common in Romania, including the widespread use of prong and electric collars, how behind the times they were and how change could be implemented. He and Kratu got on like a house on fire (Kratu can always sniff out special people) and our hour or so together put me in a really good mood. Here was someone who 'got it' and was working so hard to change perceptions and training methods. As with my experience at the university, it filled me with joy to meet a young Romanian with such drive and energy for making changes.

All of which made for quite the contrast when we got to Cluj-Napoca International Airport. A major shift from the sublime to the ridiculous. Despite his lovely manners, Kratu was looked on with judgement and coldness, further highlighting how different our countries' respective attitudes to dogs still were and reminding me how much work there was to do. One of the airport staff, in particular, couldn't hide her disdain, stepping back as we approached, but not in fear. She looked down her nose at Kratu as if he was a bad smell.

My fire was immediately fuelled by this, my baroness blood boiling. *How dare she!* I just about managed not to say anything, but the look I threw her did the job just as well – she stepped back and moved on pretty swiftly.

It was only a short note of sourness, however. From the moment we boarded the plane, we were treated like royalty. One of the air stewards immediately rushed up to greet us, eager to tell us that he had formerly been one of Alina Rusu's students and was beyond excited to have him on board.

The positive power of social media didn't extend to the arrivals hall at Luton, however, where it seemed entry back into the UK might be denied Kratu as the border staff couldn't locate his microchip. It was very late, we were very tired and this was the last thing we needed.

Useful as they are, microchips can be problematic due to their tendency to migrate within a dog's body. And when you compound that with a reader that they then admitted had an almost-dead battery, you're guaranteed to have a problem. Rattled now – and fast approaching the end of my mental tether – I suggested tersely that maybe *I* should be the one to look for it.

I eventually found it, but only at the expense of my composure, which was already shredding, because I'd had a text from a by-now heavily pregnant Scarlett to let me know she'd arrived to meet me (plus her partner, Jesse, and her dog, Bonnie) but that, not wishing to pay the eye-watering fees for short-term parking – or trudge all the way to the terminal – she had apparently parked up in some far-flung corner of one of the long-stay multistoreys.

Multistorey car parks are one of the more tedious of my various nemeses. And that's true even of the ones that I know, let alone one of those dark, scary, concrete airport monoliths. But with great sensitivity, as I told him I didn't think I could navigate my way there on my own, the ground staff manager immediately offered to escort us. And he did; with me holding Kratu and him pulling my case, he took us the entire way. I have nothing but praise and gratitude for the staff at Luton Airport, despite the 'lost' microchip fiasco.

I was also grateful to be finally bound for home and bed. There was such a lot to process, so many new ideas to implement, so strong a sense of the possibilities that could come out of what we'd seen and heard – all opening up, one by one, like happy petals. As for the dog at the centre of it all, this humble rescue boy who'd now made history, he was simply happy to settle down and go to sleep. But not before doing a magnificent sneeze, showering the Ted Baker bag I'd given Scarlett from Pup Aid in a film of saliva.

My daughter, busy navigating out of the car park now, had heard but couldn't see.

A lucky break, I decided, as I gently dabbed the designer bag – and definitely no tale-telling from me.

CHAPTER 20

European Advocate

Facebook, sometimes, has a lot to answer for. Well, more accurately, perhaps, it was more the amount of time I spent on the platform, keeping up with the output of the various groups I followed who were involved in dog rescue and raising awareness for change.

One post in particular jumped out immediately: the premiere of a film about the homeless dogs of Romania, which was to be screened at the end of November 2018 at the European Parliament in Brussels. It could hardly fail to. After all, it was something that meant so much to me; I'd seen with my own eyes how enormous the problem was and the extent of the flaws in the Romanian rescue system (both here in the UK and in Romania). There was also the small matter that sitting right beside me was a dog, a *Romanian rescue dog*, who was arguably the best ambassador and advocate for them all. So, I decided he should attend the film screening and represent them.

I looked at Kratu, and he looked back at me.

'Mr Kratu,' I said, 'I was thinking we might take a little road trip. What do you think?'

His eyes twinkling, his curiosity piqued by my own, he looked back at me with the expression of infinite wisdom reserved for such important times as this. He resonated with Adventure Tess; he loved an adventure.

I'm game if you are, his look seemed to imply.

Now all I had to do was to make this come into being. I wasn't sure if assistance dogs were allowed into the European Parliament, but if not, this one would be – I'd make sure of it. Soon the research cogs started whirring. I typed 'European Parliament access' into the search box and we were off.

Why make history once if you can make history twice, after all?

The months following my second trip to Romania had been both busy and instructive. As promised, Ray Dorgelo had come to visit in May and his talk at Wood Green had been a great success. Everyone at the charity agreed that the knowledge and information he'd shared would be an enormous help when working with these dogs in the future.

I was also hard at work trying to spread the word more generally. I'd seen and learned so much that I felt could be of benefit going forward. And change was desperately needed to stem the tide of failed rehomings, which was steadily becoming an insurmountable issue. These dogs and puppies were obviously brought to the UK with the best intentions, but were all too often ill-equipped for life in family homes. As a result, UK rescue centres were struggling to cope with the influx of foreign rescue dogs.

I was equally clear what was needed to solve the problem: education, both about what made these dogs tick and about how to train and care for them more compassionately, and better understand their needs. So, I spent a lot of time trying to drum up enthusiasm and support for the kind of changes that I knew could start making a difference; trying to get people onside with a simple and effective message that teaching was key, of both the trainers in Romania and the prospective owners here in the UK.

Sadly, my eyes were soon opened. Though there was a great deal of engagement with my ideas on social media, the people who actually acted on those words and were prepared, as Ray had been, to do something tangible seemed to be few and far between. It all began to feel very dispiriting.

Meanwhile, in what felt like a parallel life now, one particular Romanian rescue dog continued to attract the attention of the world. Though for very different, and much happier, reasons. I was by now regularly going on social media and seeing the comments about Kratu's antics at Crufts piling up – on one day I was faced with 23,000 of them! It was a mammoth task to respond to them all, but I tried my very best. Such kindness deserved it, after all. And I did, 'liking', 'loving' or replying to every comment – at least until the various platforms' headquarters put me into social media jail for doing it too quickly, making them think I was a robot. (Clearly my autistic superpower speeds were not appreciated by the powers that be in Silicon Valley ...)

It was almost too much to take in though. And too ethereal a world to risk getting lost in, so while I appreciated every single person who reached out to me and Kratu, normality, for me, was my simple life with my dogs. I was soon back to doing what I loved doing best now: walking them, training them, playing and having fun with them, and, of course, adding to my wall of rosettes.

There is a Toltec teaching which sums up how I felt at that time:

A warrior takes his lot, whatever it may be, and accepts it in ultimate humbleness. He accepts it in humbleness for what he is, not as grounds for regret, but as a living challenge.

That was me: I was a warrior. No regrets about who I was, only faith in the future I was carving out with Kratu, a soul who was the perfect example of that teaching.

By June we had reached an astonishing milestone: Kratu's antics at Crufts had amassed 10 million views. Having always had so little self-confidence and self-esteem, this felt like a truly remarkable thing. Because *I* had brought this about; I had created the circumstances and situation whereby my boy could be known and loved by millions of people.

It set me to thinking about my life and where it had taken me, and it really did seem as if I was living two separate lives. One where I was banging my head against a brick wall about rescue and corruption, hearing so much talk but seeing so little in terms of action, and the other one where, without ever even meaning to, I was showing the whole world what could be achieved when you did it right.

It was a eureka moment, but it had definitely not been my intention. At every stage I had simply followed where Kratu had led. There is another Toltec teaching which makes perfect sense to me:

What we need to do to allow magic to get hold of us is to banish doubts from our minds. Once doubts are banished anything is possible.

I had banished my doubts and Kratu was the magic that had got hold of me. And if anything was possible, and I believed that it was now, my intention was set: the European Parliament were going to let this extraordinary assistance dog through their doors.

Fortuitously, a few days after seeing the Facebook piece about the film screening, I found myself at an event where Peter Egan was also in attendance, plus Dominic Dyer, another animal advocate and wildlife protection campaigner, who my research had revealed would also be present at the EU premiere at the end of November.

I say 'fortuitously'. Some Prussian general strategy might have been involved, to be fair. (And a bit of slippery South London street-smart savvy ...) But, having become so determined that Kratu and I must be at that gathering, I was anxious to have my mission confirmed as being not completely outside the bounds of possibility.

Luckily, Dominic Dyer was at the bar when Kratu and I arrived – I recognised him immediately from his pictures on social media. Shoulders back, head held high, adopting an air of confidence I didn't feel, I walked over to him. Kratu, as ever, was just one step ahead of me, excited at the prospect of meeting a new human. And Dominic didn't disappoint. He was incredibly gentle and Kratu lapped it up; they instantly hit it off and as Dominic squatted down to make a fuss of him, Kratu rolled over on his back for a tummy tickle from his new favourite person.

I took the opportunity to sketch out my idea for us attending the screening, given Kratu was, without a shadow of a doubt, *the* poster boy for Romanian rescue. I half-expected Dominic to hum and haw, but he didn't: 'I think that's a wonderful idea,' was what he said, to my delight.

As did Peter Egan, almost word for word, some twenty minutes later when Kratu nabbed him as he was passing our table: 'You should speak to Maria Slough,' he said. 'She's the director of the film.'

Which I duly did, the next day, after tracking her down on social media. Maria also offered to find out about Kratu gaining access to Parliament and even told me she had a friend who might be happy to drive us down there.

'What, all the way to *Brussels*?'

'Yes, all the way to Brussels. She's really experienced at driving in Europe and I'm sure she'd love to go to the meeting. I'll have a word with her and get back to you as soon as I can.'

I mean, *really*? It was hard to believe the evidence of my own ears. Such incredible kindness, I was completely overwhelmed.

Sandra Kovac, Maria Slough's friend, was Slovenian. She lived in West London and though by day she did something complicated (well, to me) with computers, she devoted most of her free time to supporting animal-related causes and was a tireless campaigner for animal rights. And Maria had been right: Sandra was happy to take us and managed to get the time off from work, so on the morning of 20 November, she picked me up from my mother's house in Hertford and no sooner had she climbed out of her car than Kratu immediately jumped into it – he just *knew*. He then clambered into the back seat and settled down with our luggage, preparing to cram in as much beauty sleep as he could, knowing he had a starring role coming up. His case, by the way, was at least as big as mine. His Photizo (red light therapy is brilliant for relaxation and aching muscles, especially after a long car journey), his food, bowls and brushes. His treats and his toys, and his rose and bergamot scented refreshing body mist by Hownd (Kratu not only smells the roses in life, he smells *of* them too).

As for me, I was as prepared as I could ever be. After my experience in Cluj-Napoca earlier in the year, I had researched accommodation options carefully, eventually finding a two-bedroom apartment that, after some negotiation, agreed to take the 'celebrity' Kratu and was only a short taxi ride from the European Parliament.

To my surprise, I found my level of anxiety had changed. It had been subtle, spread over time, but I was beginning to realise that I was meeting challenges like these with a good deal less stress; I was good at it, I liked a challenge and instead of seeing nothing but impossibilities and obstacles, my perception was now that these challenges could – and would – be met. What had happened to me? Kratu had; I loved going on adventures with him, basically. It was exciting, energising, fun. His enthusiasm enthused me. His effervescence was infectious. Being out with Kratu, exploring what the world had to offer, was a little like having highs, but without taking drugs. It was a major revelation.

Unfortunately, another rather less welcome revelation revealed itself early on in our journey. When driving, Sandra liked to play music. Loud music, rock music – though the genre didn't matter. Any music, played loudly, is hard for me. The trouble was, she was driving. And she'd been *so* kind to take me. I spent the first hour in an agony of indecision, weighing up whether I should say something or not.

One of the biggest aspects of having autistic sensory overload is the difficulty it can cause when you go into an environment where there are multiple sensory stimuli bombarding your brain. And when anxiety turns to panic, one response – and often my one – is to simply leave the situation and walk away. Sometimes you can't control your environment, however, and this was clearly one of those times. But could I pluck up sufficient courage to tell her?

In the end, I knew I had to. We were less than an hour into a four- or five-hour journey and already I could feel anxiety accelerating in my chest, the urge to flee becoming a rising pressure inside my head. I could not flee a moving car, however, so I had to tell her for fear that I'd completely explode, which was the very last thing I wanted to happen. I never mean to do it, because so often people mistake my reaction for raging anger, when in reality it's just extreme frustration with myself that I don't feel worthy enough to be allowed to express needs.

I think it stems back to my childhood and adolescence. When your voice isn't heard when you're young it can affect you deeply; you begin to feel as if you don't deserve a voice. Needless to say, as an adult I'd rather jump off a mountain than have those confrontations. If I think I might offend someone, I crumble inside then out it all explodes and I end up doing it anyway.

It took me almost until Folkestone to gather up that courage and when I did say something, she could not have been nicer. 'Oh, you should have *said*!' she told me. 'It's *fine*. I understand, please don't worry.' And in the bliss of the sudden quiet I could only sit and marvel at her kindness and goodness and empathy. And then felt bad about subjecting her to such a long, tuneless drive, and then, once I'd processed all of *that*, just so incredibly grateful.

Sandra, I still am, to this day.

Things didn't get any easier when we arrived. We needed to find somewhere to eat – I knew my blood sugar was low and if I didn't eat, my nausea would be even worse – and finding somewhere that would accommodate Kratu was challenging. For one reason or another, I kept saying no to everywhere we looked at, and once again, I know I must have driven Sandra mad. Her patience with me was amazing. But we eventually found a place close to the European Parliament building and after a meal, including a much-needed glass of wine for me and some tasty tidbits from our meal for Kratu, it was time to go and make another bit of history.

The European Parliament building was obviously impressive, but it was dark and I didn't see any of it. I was also much too busy watching where my feet were going as I was terrified of falling arse over tit back down the stone steps – which would hurt. And was not the entrance I wanted to make.

With its multiple flags standing to attention outside, there was no doubting the importance and gravitas of the place. But it was the people gathered at the top of the steps who caught my gaze and one in particular, who seemed to shine like a beacon of happy light. The tall, inspiring shape of Peter Egan. To see his smiling face – someone I recognised – was just the tonic I needed and to see the delight with which he stooped down to welcome Kratu, I felt a huge whoosh of relief and gratitude course through me.

'You made it!' he said, and as we followed him inside, I felt so proud. My Kratu was walking up the stairs to the European Parliament. My goodness, what an honour – we'd done it!

I was so overcome with emotion that I had tears in my eyes.

I was crying for a different reason once the film had been aired. It was something I'd anticipated, of course, because I'd seen the stark reality for Romania's stray dogs for myself, but it didn't lessen the impact of that thirty or so minutes, both for me and for everyone present. Most chilling was one of the final scenes where one of the activists featured came upon a dog lying by a road, near one of the 'shelters'. The animal was plainly terrified, shaking and whimpering in terror, but unable to run away because it could no longer move. It had already been injected with the paralysing drug that would eventually kill it – an agonising and truly horrible death.

Seeing that part, in particular, really reinforced for me that I'd been right to avoid going to any 'kill' shelters. Because that was what they were – as one of the contributors to the film said, they were a kind of 'state-sanctioned Auschwitz for dogs'. I knew then that had I been to one of these shelters, I would not have been able to contain myself. If I'd seen a human hurt a dog, I would have stepped in and more than likely ended up being hurt myself.

There was an antidote to the feelings of fury and revulsion, however. The fact that we were seeing it. That I was surrounded by people who cared enough to want to do something about it. That in my passion for helping these dogs I wasn't alone. I also felt a huge welling of gratitude, both for me and for Kratu. And felt the contrast even more deeply than I had before; here he was, sitting eating chicken treats at the European Parliament while people – such good people – were discussing what they could do to ensure other dogs just like him had the chance of the happier life they so deserved.

After the screening and discussion there was an 'aftershow' gathering at a nearby hotel, laid on for everyone who had attended. Including Kratu, of course, who was delighted to be attending his first cocktail party and to be made such a fuss of by everyone.

We didn't stay long, though. I was genuinely much too tired and emotional, and I knew Kratu was similarly drained. But when we got back to the apartment I remembered the little bottle of Prosecco I still had stashed away in my case. While Sandra snored in her room, and Kratu sprawled on my bed, I sat in the little living room and opened it. And before I sipped, I toasted the universe for bringing me Kratu and for bringing us to this incredible point.

I then raised a glass to my other soulmate: his mother, Tutty.

CHAPTER 21

The Uncommon Dog

What I'd seen and heard on the EU trip stayed with me for days afterwards. I try hard to keep out of the politics of rescue, but I was haunted by the image of that dog dying in agony by the road. I know some people say charity should always begin at home and why adopt a dog from abroad with all the complications that entails when there are dogs that can be adopted here at home? And they have a point. But, for me at least, that argument is beside the point. This was about helping a suffering animal, full stop. Where there is cruelty you need to put a halt to it, full stop. It doesn't matter where it happens, because compassion for animals shouldn't see national boundaries: cruelty is cruelty.

Being in the presence of all those welfare advocates with Kratu really made me think about that and it took me a long while to process. It felt such an amazing honour to be present in the first place and also reinforced my belief that we should speak up and speak out about animal welfare, making the necessary changes in law so animals can be protected.

Which was what led me and Kratu to APDAWG.

APDAWG stands for the All-party Parliamentary Dog Advisory Welfare Group. It was set up in 2017 to support charities and campaigners involved in dog health and welfare and to give them a voice in Westminster. I already knew a little about it as I followed some of its key supporters on social media, including Peter Egan, of course, whom I'd just seen in Brussels, and the vet Marc Abraham (Marc the Vet), whom I'd also met a few times now at celebrity dog shows. After our trip to the EU Parliament, and having now met some highly motivated and passionate people, I was more driven than ever to contribute what I could to support the vital work they were all doing, so when I saw a Facebook post by Marc about an upcoming meeting, it dawned on me that, if they'd let us, Kratu and I should try to attend this as well.

Mainly, I was keen to educate myself. I wanted to know more about animal welfare generally, more about the existing laws that were in place to protect animals, and what I could do to support the causes and to help bring about the change that was so important to protect animals.

Kratu was key here. He had become my right-hand dog. It was the best kind of positive feedback loop in that without me, he wouldn't have been able to have all these adventures and without *him*, I would never have been able to do anything remotely like this – travelling, meeting strangers, making such difference as I could. Our human–canine bond was not only incredibly deep but also mutually beneficial.

The meeting, which was taking place just before Christmas 2018, was one of their regular ones dedicated to 'unsung heroes'. These were centred on celebrating a particularly inspiring person or dog welfare group, and this one was to honour an amazing little boy called Owen Howkins and his huge three-legged rescue dog, Haatchi. Both dog and boy had faced considerable physical challenges. Haatchi, an Anatolian Shepherd dog, had to have his leg amputated after being dumped on a railway track in North London and hit by a train, while Owen suffers from the rare genetic condition of Schwartz-Jampel syndrome, or SJS. It's a humbling and heart-rending story.

I got in touch with Marc Abraham and he told me how to apply to be present at the meeting – I just needed to write to Parliament to get permission from the Serjeant at Arms, which was quickly agreed. Then came the hard part. Another trip into central London with Kratu – something I already knew, after my experience doing the Sky panel show *Duck Quacks Don't Echo*, could be challenging on several fronts. It was also some distance from Liverpool Street to Westminster and there was no way I'd contemplate taking Kratu on the Underground. What if he got his big hairy paws stuck in the escalator? What if the train was caught in a tunnel? Plus, it was approaching Christmas and London would be teeming with people.

There was nothing for it: I would need to get a taxi. Trouble was I had only so much money, so I'd need to do some subliminal programming on both taxi and taxi driver if we were going to arrive under my £15 budget. We did a great job, pulling up outside Portcullis House with £12.90 on the clock! Don't ask me how, that's classified information.

We disembarked and I took Kratu for a wee along the Embankment. *Come on, Mr Kratu, let's do this*, I whispered as we walked up the steps to the entrance to the building, where I had already been warned we'd both be patted down and searched.

As ever, Kratu took this in his stride. Where I saw two big imposing police officers, he merely saw new friends. If he could, I'm quite sure he would have thanked them for their attentions.

He soon touched them with his mesmerising gaze – guaranteed to warm even the hearts of big burly policemen – and managed to elicit a couple of smiles in return. But only small ones; this is serious security and rightly so.

All checks completed, a woman then showed us both to the staircase which would lead to the room where the meeting was to be held. Oh no, I thought, because I could see there were treads but no risers, so you could see through the gap. And so could Kratu, who proceeded to consider the stairs with a head tilt to one side, then the other and an eye roll.

Here we go, I thought, as he did a strange walk up the stairs – his new *Crouching Tiger, Hidden Dragon* stealth mode; he's suspicious of stairs you can see between. (Maybe if the spaces between the stairs couldn't see him, he couldn't see them either. I'm never completely sure of his motivation but we made it.)

We sat down and waited as we were early (being late is a great fear of mine) but were soon joined by a woman who had also arrived early and who immediately knelt down and made a huge fuss of Kratu. She introduced herself as Ariana Williams and told me she already knew Kratu from Facebook.

Ariana, who was a veterinary patient care assistant (PCA) and an active member of APDAWG, couldn't have appeared at a better time because I had no idea what the procedure was or where to go. I had more than a fluttering of butterflies in my stomach – I had moths, dragonflies, locusts, those weird weevil-type beetles and possibly a couple of pterodactyls as well! Anything that flew, I decided, was definitely in there so to spend a few moments being distracted couldn't have been more helpful right then.

Once in the chamber, however, all thoughts of my anxiety disappeared. It was, as I'd anticipated, an intensely moving experience as Peter Egan told the story of Owen and Haatchi's friendship and when Owen himself spoke, there wasn't a dry eye in the house. To see that small boy and his enormous dog, and hear how they supported one another, made for an incredibly powerful meeting. And the bond shared by Owen and his canine companion resonated with me on a very deep level: it just felt so right that my own bond with Kratu had brought me to this place where I could honour another deep human–animal connection.

I did, however, begin to feel the day catching up on me as the meeting began drawing to a close. The train journey, the taxi ride, making it into Westminster and going through all the security procedures to get into the meeting had been exhausting.

Kratu must have clocked this and decided it was time to take me home. He led me towards the door and though I stopped briefly to speak to Peter Egan, he was not taking no for an answer.

'Kratu wants to go,' I told Peter as he held my hand in greeting.

'Quite,' he said, smiling. 'I completely understand,' as Kratu gently guided me along and out of the door, as he was trained to at times when I was overwhelmed, in order to get me to an exit. At least this time we found a lift. Hurrah! No more *Crouching Tiger* stairs.

By the time we'd emerged back out on to the street, it was now dark and very cold. As if sensing my overload, Kratu continued in 'get Mum home' mode. We flagged down a taxi and Kratu was the first inside. I followed gratefully and sank down into the seat, oblivious to what was going on outside the cab. This was the thick of the rush hour, plus it was also approaching Christmas, but if there were fairy lights and Christmas trees and shoppers and tourists, I don't recall any of it – I was just grateful to arrive back at Liverpool Street station with enough money left for some sushi. It was then carefully back up the stone steps and down into the station, where I also wanted to pick up a mini bottle of Prosecco.

I had to take over here as Kratu wanted to get straight on the train, but I was getting something to eat and drink and that was the end of it (well, I need the occasional high-value treat too). We then found the gate and by a whisker made the train I'd booked a seat on.

While I sipped on the Prosecco, Kratu lying on the floor beside me, the train hurtled its way towards home and I felt a sense of contentment come over me. That was a huge step with self-confidence and in trust and faith in Kratu. And I had met a lovely lady, Ariana. This was a good thing, indeed. New experiences, new people and I was safe now with Kratu. Reaching down, I offered him a piece of salmon sushi, which he took, but then promptly spat out again. That was fine. I never much liked the look of his dinner either – if I'd tried it, I would probably have spat it out too.

But the food for thought was almost as delicious as the sushi as I took in another mind-blowing moment. All my life I'd had such a horror of going to new places, yet here I was, fresh off the back of attending the European Parliament, actually returning from the nerve centre of the UK one now as well. What had happened to me?

Kratu, that's what. This dog of mine had taken me to places I could never have imagined going, *ever*. He'd taken my fears and insecurities and basically wrapped himself around them – a bit like a pair of tweezers firmly gripping a splinter, swiftly yanking out the source of pain and allowing the wound to heal. Splinter by splinter, he was restoring me to the person I could have been: the person I now knew I could be.

CHAPTER 22

Adversity and Heartache

Because it's the sort of thing that happens in everyone's life sometimes, my euphoria about my visit to the APDAWG meeting at Westminster was soon followed by a plunge into the cold waters of harsh reality and my equilibrium, always fragile at the best of times, took a tumble.

It was Maia. My haughty wolf dog was becoming an old lady, so when she started slowing down and gaining weight, I didn't worry too much at first; I was slowing down and gaining weight myself, after all. The vet agreed; yes, they could do some blood tests if I liked, but he didn't see anything to worry about unduly.

Then one day in late December one of the other dogs accidentally knocked against Maia and to my shock, she screamed, obviously in great pain. I ran straight over to comfort her and it felt as if her stomach was distended. Oh, dear heavens, I thought, please don't let this be bloat. Back in the car, back to the vet's and this time it was different. Not bloat, but something equally terrifying and sinister: she had a very large tumour on her spleen.

The only option, I was told, was to operate immediately. And if she was riddled with cancer, would I be prepared for them to let her go? *No, no, no!* If it was, then they must bring her back round so she could spend her final time on earth nestled in my arms and go peacefully, knowing I was there with her.

It was so huge a thing to contemplate that I was lost for a while. The tears fell in a torrent, my heart was swollen with sadness. As I drove home from the vet's without her I could do nothing but climb inside to the centre of the shitstorm.

My heart had been broken many times, many pieces lost because of grief or sadness, and other unknown emotions I couldn't process or handle. I now had to examine what *this* was. And I realised it wasn't heartbreak but heart*ache*. My heart was not going to break this time as I had a grasp now on what love was. If I lost Maia, now or later, what I must do was give thanks for my most extraordinary, slightly wild, aloof, wolfy girl. Who had had my back through chemo, who had got me through those last years in London. Who had got me *out* of London and my old life. Who had led me to Paqo, then Kratu.

She was, undoubtedly, the most beautiful wolf girl in the world, nothing short of magnificent. I was going to be so grateful, so happy she had been in my life. Whatever happened, I was going to replace that swollen grief-filled heart with pure love for her.

I thought of my beliefs and how much they mattered to me. Some see me as very detached and cold, which is typically autistic, but is also a Toltec practice: the more you can release and let go, the freer you are, and it comes back down to putting in the effort to change your perception and let go of your past.

I had collected a great deal of heavy energy in the past as I hadn't released things I'd felt and been through and let go. Now, as I was aware of the heavy energy stuck inside me, I did one of the Q'ero energy clearing techniques I had learned and released it, so I could keep the happy energy flowing and moving forward.

And I now knew, without doubt, why I could do this. Kratu had spent a lot of time practising *kintsugi* with my heart, carefully gluing back all the lost and broken pieces, making it much stronger and more resilient than it had ever been. It was now a restored vessel, one that contained a lot of love.

What Kratu had done for me was a huge revelation. In the centre of that shitstorm, suddenly I could smell the roses and whatever happened, I was going to celebrate Maia's magnificence. I would focus all my energies on what an absolute pleasure it had been to have her in my life. This was the way I was determined to process it. Every time I felt like crying during those interminable few hours, I had to pull myself back and say *no!* Magnificence, gratitude. Those two words became my mantra. I would be strong for her.

I am not religious but I do pray – to the universe, to Mother Earth, to all my ancestors. And, my goodness, as I waited, I prayed so hard. Eventually the call came to tell me I was allowed to go and get her. In those scant seconds between hearing that and how the operation had gone, I think I prayed even harder. But it had been successful, the vet told me. They had removed both Maia's spleen and her tumour, and though only time would tell, they were hopeful, she added, that the cancer was all contained within it.

Once I got Maia home I asked friends across the world to work along with me, working with light, the Andean healing way of accelerating combined energies from Mother Earth and the cosmos. I did this now and as I lay my hands on her, the other dogs had all come close and lay around her.

Stepping back and seeing that brought a lump to my throat. It was so emotionally charged, such a manifestation of love, and there was such a sense of peace and tranquillity in the room. I stood in the doorway and took a couple of photos, one of which had this unexplained column of light running through it, from the top down to the site of her operation.

I kept the photo. Whether or not you believe in what I believe in, or what I do, *I* know. And that's all that matters.

Maia duly recovered. Her scans were all clear. The cancer had gone. It hadn't been her time yet. And, in time, she returned to her normal grumpy, aloof, old-lady, greedy, wolfy self and I have never been so relieved to have her back to normal.

Even if it did mean nearly losing my finger each time she took a treat.

Meanwhile, back in Kratu Land, I was wondering, would he or wouldn't he? As in would he do the Agility course we'd trained for or would he perform his by now legendary freestyling at Crufts 2019, which was rapidly approaching. And wondering was all I could do, because it didn't matter how much we practised, I really had given up the ghost of trying to work out his Machiavellian Plots of Great Cunning to scupper my hard work at Agility performances.

He'd also started his own resistance movement. I'd begun to notice that every time we returned home from a journey, he would refuse to get out of the car. There was an irony there. What a long way we'd come from the time when I didn't want to go *anywhere*, because now I was clearly showing him such a good time that he never wanted to go home; he was just always so up for adventure.

Unfortunately, however, it wasn't just Kratu who did this – he had shown the Way of Resistance to my other dogs too, which meant getting in the house became a major exercise.

I had long ago removed my rear seats so the dogs had more

room and Kratu's Resistance HQ was always the rear footwell. From here, he would direct operations, instigating a mass sit-in – *we shall not be moved!* – and all the other dogs quickly followed his lead. Kratu was the worst, Raffy always a very close second, then Paqo and then lastly, Polo – who used to be more biddable and would come out when I called, until General Kratu soon put a stop to it.

Most days I'd manage to coax the other dogs in eventually, but Kratu, always holding on to the last for another trip, could not even be bribed out with treats. Sometimes, I'd even have to leave him out there, him looking out of the window, pretending he didn't recognise me. Other times, he'd look straight into my eyes: *Who are you, strange woman? I do not know you.*

I at least figured out how to catch him out. If I waited round the corner in a place where he couldn't see me, he'd immediately jump straight back up onto the rear cushions. I could then sneak up like a ninja, bent over double, then fling the door open. I would then win and he would agree to come out. He'd have a grin on his face reminiscent of the Cheshire Cat. I'd grin right back at him. Being such a copycat, what else would I do?

We had been meeting Wendy regularly in the run-up to the show and doing some practising in Wood Green's big arena hall. It had the same flooring as at Crufts, which was always good for the dogs to practise on, and both Kratu and Polo had been doing amazingly well. Polo was learning to follow with great direction and focus, while Kratu was doing jumps with great skill and pomposity – he could never do a jump now without an exuberant 'woof!' *Look at me!* he seemed to say. *Aren't I brilliant?*

Still, it remained to be seen whether that would translate into his moment in the Crufts spotlight – which they were already billing as a not-to-be-missed highlight, even featuring him in the build-up in their online magazine. No pressure, then.

This time, it was also going to be a whole weekend away. Kratu was by now a brand ambassador for Photizo red light therapy, so after our appearance on the Friday, we would not be going home. Instead, we were booked into a local hotel and would spend Saturday and Sunday doing PR work for Photizo, as well as Natural Instinct, now a long-standing collaboration. They would be long days, I knew, but I put them out of my mind. We had Kratu's third Crufts appearance to do first. Third time lucky? Much as I'd loved how his freestyling antics had been received at the first two, there was a little part of me that would have loved it had he done a proper course, just so the world could see what he *could* do.

But, of course, that was never going to happen. Kratu is always excited when a trip in the car is on the cards, but on the morning of Crufts, when Wendy arrived to pick us up, he was bubbling away like a steam engine, clearly keen to get going. Was he already thinking about the fun that lay ahead?

Evidently yes, because when we got into the arena that afternoon, Kratu went off in his own freestyle bonanza straight away. He did one token jump for me, then bounded straight off into the tunnel. I couldn't see what he was up to but already I could hear the audience laughing, so he was presumably up to some mischief in there. When I got to the tunnel I'm sure he was laughing at me. He came out and did another jump for me, but then he spotted Wendy standing by the exit and bounded over to say hello to her, then to the ladies who sit and help, then over another couple of jumps (he was freestyling now, big time), then – *ah, there it is!* – back into the tunnel, where he lay down and waited for me, as if to say '*Na na na! You can't catch me!*', then out, over the A frame and back *again* into the tunnel.

'Where are you?' I called.

'*Boo!*' He had turned and come out the same end he went in.

The crowd was going wild and he was lapping it up now. This was what he'd come for and you could sense his pride and pleasure in performing. He did a beautiful extended trot along the ringside, sniffing all the people, looking up at them, and then a quick spurt of galloping around, a 'WOOF!' over a final jump, then sauntered out of the arena, head held high. Ah, but wait – there was something missing ... *Me!* So, he trotted back, scooped me up and back off we went, applause and laughter ringing in my ears.

Who had wanted him to do a proper course, anyway? I thought. No one. They had wanted Kratu to be Kratu and once again, he'd delivered.

It was delivering of a different kind that faced us for the next two days. With the other dogs safely at home and relaxing with Ergun, Kratu and I spent the weekend meeting and greeting, going up and down between the stands of Photizo and Natural Instinct so many times that we could probably have walked the route between Halls 1 and 3 of Crufts blindfolded.

By the Sunday afternoon, I was exhausted so it was fortunate that I'd been able to secure a lift home from Penny Roberts, a hugely respected Samoyed owner and dog show judge who had awarded Kratu two Best in Shows in one memorable Scamps dog show back in 2017. She has a big soft spot for Kratu and we'd been friends ever since.

The only trouble was that I now had to find her. She was

stewarding at Crufts and could be anywhere. I spent some agonising minutes trying to work out in my frazzled brain how exactly I was going to track her down.

Logic prevailed, though. When in doubt about something, ask questions. I finally managed to ask the right question of the right person, eventually knocking on the door of the steward control centre (or whatever they call it) and of course they knew exactly where she was – they had an enormous board and a lot of notes. After inspecting a few entries, the man said, 'Yes! Here she is!' – she was in the ring where they were judging Chihuahuas. And had been less than thirty metres from me all day.

They were finishing up by the time Kratu and I got to her and I couldn't have been more pleased to see her. I was even more pleased when she commented that she was done in too and very happy to make a speedy getaway. (Well, as speedy as it could be, given the amount of stuff we were both carrying!)

And I say 'speedy'. Penny is notorious for her sense of direction. Or lack of ... She openly admits that anyone who has ever been in a car with her knows her sense of direction is terrible. As I found out. It took three turns around the car park before we finally made it out, but we got out eventually and then she surprised me: 'Right,' she said. 'Just so you know, Tess ...'

She went on to explain that there would be no chit-chat on the drive home because driving was a serious business and that Radio 5 Live would be playing for the duration of the journey, even if it was something as boring as the cricket results. She said it helped her concentration.

Well, she couldn't have had a more appreciative passenger. Not just because she'd been so kind driving Kratu and me back from Crufts but also because I understood exactly where she was coming from and admired her confidence and frankness in saying so. So,

I shut up and couldn't help but smile to myself: perhaps Penny wasn't so different from me after all.

Kratu slept the entire way (slow and steady, on this journey, won the motorway race) but once we arrived at Penny's house, he was up on his paws in an instant. We had to go inside and wait for Ergun, who was on his way to collect us, and while we waited he was treated to a dose of doggy heaven as he was greeted by her two beautiful Samoyeds. Two gorgeous clouds of white fur, Penny's dogs were the canine equivalent of Las Vegas showgirls, wafting their voluminous tails all around him, both with their huge Samoyed smiles.

So, Kratu got to do what he'd been wanting to do all weekend, but couldn't, because all the dogs were at a distance: sniff two beautifully white, very furry, very friendly bitches in the kind of proper greeting (and the politest information exchange) dogs can do. And, fair enough, he couldn't have encountered two more beautiful butts so he sniffed deeply, delight written all over his face.

Personally, I preferred their other ends – they were such beautiful animals, proper pedigrees, with the most delightful temperament – but I wasn't sorry when Ergun pulled up shortly afterwards to drive us back home because what I most wanted to greet now was a large glass of wine – a high-value reward for a high-stress couple of days. And however Mr Kratu might feel about the matter, it's better than sniffing a butt – even a pedigree butt – any day!

CHAPTER 23

Safe to Be Me

Kratu's third outing at Crufts, just like the others, went viral. Countries all around the world were now showing and sharing Kratu, from indie websites to some of the big media platforms: The Dodo, LADbible, the leading newspapers and magazines, even *Time* magazine did a piece on him.

This time he even caught the attention of a legendary Australian broadcaster, Ozzy Man. I'd already come across Ozzy Man Reviews... after the previous Crufts, when someone suggested he should review Kratu's performance. Then I googled him – he does reviews for all sorts of events and happenings – and even for me, with my no-nonsense South London sensibilities, his language was a little on the 'out there' side of 'out there'.

I wasn't sure some of Kratu's fans would approve. Still, it wasn't up to me and he did a spectacular review of Kratu's round, which was hilarious and impressed me greatly, and as everyone else seemed to embrace his colourful language as much as I did, added several more million views to his total. Everyone loves an underdog, especially one as personable, intelligent and entertaining as Kratu, and it seemed my hairy honey monster was by now becoming something of a canine international treasure.

As before, though, life at home carried on much the same. However lovely it was to know the world had taken Kratu to their hearts, what was even more important to me was how our own bond was blossoming. By now we were having conversations in which actions, and the physical input Kratu brought, were just as important as words, if not more so. Actions often *can* speak louder than words and Kratu was proving this to me daily. He had this thing where he'd stare at me until he had my full attention and when I'd say 'What?', he'd swivel with his hips and plop his bearbum onto my lap or one knee. He'd then look at me over his shoulder and make funny huffs, blowing out his cheeks and making gentle huffing noises.

It was such a happy noise – one of pure joy, signalling that he wanted to engage me in play. I would always stroke him when he did this and tell him how much I loved him. He'd reply with a chuff and a woof before getting up again and doing his play-bow, his bearbum up in the air.

Come on, he'd imply. *Time to go out*. And on some days, my particularly anxious days, this wasn't just a joy, it was a necessity if I was to make it out of the front door. An invitation like this just had to be accepted and I could conquer those fears and step foot outside with my loyal companion Kratu guiding me gently to the car or for a walk. And, more often than not, an adventure.

Kratu and I would also shriek together. It made quite a racket, and had to be done in private, but was something we both enjoyed immensely. I'd lie on the floor close to him and he'd tuck his front paws up and show his chest – a clear invitation for a cuddle. I would put my head on his chest and hum loudly, enjoying the feeling of vibration and the fur tickling my face and nose. He would then put his paws either side of my head and with our faces close together, he would whistle.

This was, no question, when my mask would disappear. Autistic Tess would be allowed to give free rein to her emotions and, as we whistled and shrieked together, it was a shared special sensory indulgence. In pitch-perfect tune with each other, it was always a moment of incredible connection. A communication where two species were making the same sound, both filled with joy and being the free, slightly wild spirits we both were. Such moments were – and still are – magical. I would always think afterwards that the people who didn't recognise me as autistic might think differently if they could see how I really was, with the mask off, rocking and rolling around on the floor with Kratu, behind closed doors. It was only then with my beloved boy that I felt safe to be me.

With our bond strengthening every day, we went to more dog shows, we walked and trained, and we continued to do sessions at Kettlefields, the local primary school. We'd definitely found the perfect environment for our therapy work and our visits to see the children there had become a big part of our lives now. It was something we really looked forward to and enjoyed. Finally, we had found the right niche.

That third Crufts appearance also led to some exciting opportunities. A photo shoot for a magazine campaign for a product which – ahem! – my dogs are not allowed to eat, a TV advert for the same product, which was shown in Europe (including, to my great delight, Romania), a billboard for a bank, a scene for a series called *The Curse* on Netflix and Kratu also filmed a scene for the Disney live action film, *Cruella*.

Though we didn't make the final cut, that was a really fun day out. *Cruella* was being shot on location in Buckinghamshire and everyone on set was so friendly and kind. Plus, the food was *amazing*. They had a chef grilling steaks on a big outdoor grill and though I'd already eaten when he asked me if I'd like one, what else could I say but yes please? I knew a certain someone who'd appreciate a big juicy steak, and since that someone was the one doing the hard work of acting, I felt he deserved to have one too. Though I wasn't sure anyone else would see it like that, so a certain amount of sleight of hand was required to fold it into my napkin and slip it away without anyone seeing...

Kratu was even offered a job on a new ITV series about dog training, where he had to be taught, using a clicker, to ride a skateboard. I turned that one down, though, as it was something I'd already taught him a while ago, and in ten minutes. Also, it felt all wrong to have someone 'training' him to do something he could do already, which to me seemed completely pointless, and deceptive too.

But, just as Kratu does on floor surfaces he doesn't approve of, fate moves in mysterious ways. Because the audition clip for the TV show led us to a much greater achievement in the form of a place in the line-up in the 2019 Autism's Got Talent show, which was to be held in May.

I was now growing as passionate about autism-related causes as I was about dog training and rescue, and had already come across a lady I admired called Anna Kennedy, who'd founded a small independent charity, Anna Kennedy Online. The charity's mission was to raise autism awareness and support families with autism-related challenges, and her annual talent show had been going for several years now.

I knew it was a long shot, but I was starting to believe in us now;

that we were good enough to perform tricks in front of people. Already I was winning a lot of trick classes with Kratu, so why not step it up a notch and see if we could do it on stage? So, full of enthusiasm, I sent in the audition clip and to my surprise and delight, we were accepted on to the line-up for the show. I say 'surprise' and 'delight' but the more accurate words were 'shock' and 'horror' because I hadn't actually planned on being accepted. Because this was no dog show, it was completely different territory. I had to come up with some kind of clever trick routine and not just for Kratu because for some completely unknown and daft reasoning I decided two dogs could do this and Polo was coming too. (I think I must have been feeling a bit bonkers that day; I was clearly not thinking straight at all.)

But I was committed now, so I set to work with a vengeance. I had to choreograph and practise a two-minute routine, which, let me tell you, is a long time when you're performing. So, with the help of a lovely friend called Sally Marchant (she'd helped me a few years previously with Do As I Do training), I came up with something I thought would do the trick, involving Kratu opening a door and Polo coming out of it, some hoop work and a couple of tricks on step stools, for which there were signs – 'the naughty step' and 'the goodest boy ever'. You get the picture ... My grand finale, I decided, would be my 'bang dead' trick with both of them – I'd done it a lot with the children at Kettlefields and it was their favourite trick. It was also the first trick Kratu ever learned and had been polished to perfection – he even groaned as he 'died' – so I knew I was on relatively safe ground there.

Even so, by the time May came around, I was more nervous than ever. This was appearing on stage, with all eyes just on you. Nowhere to hide, nowhere to run. And in such a prestigious location! The show took place that year at the Mermaid Theatre, close to the River Thames in Blackfriars, London, and to make everything stress-free for both the organisers and 'acts', Anna Kennedy had kindly treated us to two nights at a nearby hotel.

I was also, once again, indebted to the kindness of Sally Marchant, who offered to drive us, plus our props, down to London. Sally is a one-woman powerhouse and runs an online business called naturallyhappydogs.com, which provides expert advice for dog owners, much of it in the form of videos on YouTube, a couple of which were the genesis of two of Kratu's best tricks. They are all free, all fun and full of useful information, from behavioural insights to feeding, to breed information and training tips, presented by leading experts in their various fields. It's an incredible resource and keeps her very busy, so I was hugely grateful to her for offering to take us. (And more than a little mortified to hear that while helping me haul my props into the hotel, she'd been issued with a parking ticket for her trouble. I went into Prussian general mode and after stating my case very effectively, got it cancelled the following week. Least I could do.)

After a quiet night (well, as is possible when you're sharing a hotel room with two fidgeting canines), I woke the next morning with my anxiety in overdrive. Why had I applied to put myself through this ordeal? And why had I decided to involve Polo? Sometimes I wonder quite what goes on in my brain when I make certain decisions. But the decision was made now and there was no backing out.

And if my nerves had good reason to be jangling already, then came the news that TV personality and former model Katie Price and her son Harvey would be watching the show and their group would be sitting in the front row. I liked Katie, but I was worried about this: there was going to be a film crew in tow, as they were filming it for Katie's reality show – something that didn't bode well for any bloopers going unnoticed.

Plus, I was by now having a 'reality check moment' of my own when Kratu, who had cheekily stolen most of Polo's breakfast, developed explosive diarrhoea on our way back to the hotel after a trip to the shops to grab some lunch. There are times, let me tell you – and dog owners will relate to this – when a doggy poo bag is about as useful as a chocolate teapot. I could only slosh the contents of my bottle of spring water over it and cling to the positive that at least it had happened now, rather than on stage in the Mermaid Theatre.

It got worse. On the return to our hotel room, Kratu went to leap on the bed, with the beautiful white sheets just freshly made. I had wanted to check him over and wipe him down first, but no go – he landed on the bed, wiggling his bearbum in delight, and as he did so, painted a kind of poopy Picasso with every swish of his slightly poop-splattered tail nub.

Horrified, but thinking on my feet, I rang housekeeping, telling them I'd had something on my shoe which had made the sheets dirty. Then as soon as I put the phone down, I thought *what?* What would they think? Probably that I was the worst kind of hotel guest (well, almost). The sort who climbed up on their beds with their shoes on.

I spent the afternoon making sure Kratu had plenty of water, but absolutely nothing more to eat. We also went on regular toilet breaks, my hope being that by the time of the show, he'd be empty. The main problem, however, was that I daren't give him any treats during our routine for fear of setting myself up for an onstage re-run. Which was a problem. Kratu tries his very best when he knows there are high-value rewards and without them, things could take a turn for the worse. You never knew what mischief might ensue.

There was little I could do about it, however, and my nerves were really ramping up, so when my friend Karen arrived to do some photographs and support me (the friend who'd helped me with my autism questionnaire), it proved to be a welcome distraction. Even so, as our time onstage approached, I was beginning to wonder if *I'd* remember the routine, let alone Polo and Kratu. Remembering routines is hard at the best of times and when you're terrified – which I was – even more so. Still, I was determined to do my very best and, luckily, we were on very early as I couldn't have coped with waiting till the end.

The compère announced us and we started. Kratu had to go and sit in the box and then lie down hiding until I called him, but he had no intention of doing as he was told. He kept popping his head up and then jumped out of his own accord. Meanwhile, it was Polo's turn – spinning around with his front paws on a step. I then sent Kratu to sit on the naughty step. Except he hadn't. Unbeknown to me, but in full view of the audience, he was right behind me, following in my footsteps.

The rest of the tricks then went reasonably well. Both jumped through the hoops and Kratu did some skateboarding, but then it all started unravelling. Perhaps inspired by his brother's mutiny, Polo, to my horror, had a sudden case of the zoomies, running in circles around me as if he had a rocket up his backside – then back and forth across the stage, completely letting rip, indulging his wild side to the max.

None of which boded well for the grand finale, which was the 'bang dead' trick we'd practised to perfection. And my prediction was right: once they'd hit the deck, they decided it would be more fun to respond to my 'bang!' by bopping each other's noses with their paws – less dead dogs than a pair of boxing hares.

'Bang!' I said again. 'Bang!' They completely ignored me.

'BANG!' I said, a third time, this time much louder and, *finally*, they dropped into their 'dead' pose. As in *really* still. As in not-moving-a-single-muscle dead pose. So still were they that I wouldn't have been surprised to find they'd both gone to sleep. And perhaps they had. Maybe they were finally that exhausted. I couldn't tell you what the audience thought, because I'd not once allowed myself to even acknowledge them. I was just so, so relieved we were finished.

I only realised how monumental this was for me immediately afterwards. I had faced and conquered a huge fear. It hadn't gone to plan, but hardly anything I do with Kratu ever does, plus we'd met new people, risen to a huge challenge and survived it.

I said goodbye to Karen and by now feeling very overloaded, I tried to get something to eat. And this time without success. Despite both dogs having their assistance dog slips on, place after place took one look at them and said no. This was a real shock for me. I'd experienced it in Romania, but never once in the UK, and it saddened me greatly. I had no idea about being refused access to places and it struck me that some people faced this kind of hostility on a regular basis. I understood now and it wasn't pleasant at all.

I'd got to the point of resigning myself to a sandwich in the hotel room when the manager of the last place I tried, a little Mexican restaurant called Cheeky Chico's, surprised me by smiling and saying yes, absolutely, my own cheeky chicos were very welcome. He then led us to a table where there was plenty of room for Kratu and Polo to lie down on the floor and go to sleep.

Well, in theory. And it must have been fate, I decided, because almost as soon as I'd ordered fajitas and a glass of wine, we were approached by a woman from the adjacent table.

'Is that Kratu?' she asked in an American accent.

I was dumbfounded for a moment. Had she been at the show? Apparently not.

'From Crufts?' she added helpfully. 'Oh, I *love* him.'

She then made a huge fuss of both Kratu and Polo, explaining that she'd seen Kratu's Crufts performance on *Good Morning America* and had been following him on social media ever since.

I was deeply touched and walked back to the hotel feeling really moved by the encounter. I knew Kratu had fans from all over the world, but that was the virtual world. This had been a real-life interaction. I think we'd made her day and she had certainly made mine – I hoped it meant as much to her as it had to me.

I finished the evening with a final glass of fizz in the bar before the boys' last toilet run before bed. A lot of people wanted to stroke the dogs and have photographs with them. Buoyed up with the wine, I smiled and said yes. So daring! So unlike me! But that was what the day had done for me. Despite the various hiccups, it had been such a tremendous experience. This was not the dog world, it was the autism world and everyone we met had been so welcoming and kind. That had made *me* feel comfortable, as well as Kratu and Polo. Something rare and unusual indeed.

I went to bed that night feeling gratitude as well as huge relief. No, it hadn't been quite the routine I had planned, but the audience seemed to have enjoyed it, Kratu and Polo had had fun and I could tick another box on the 'accomplishment' list, which meant another occasion when I had conquered my fears.

A talent agent tweeted the next day that it was the best dog comedy routine they had ever seen.

CHAPTER 24

It's Okay to Cry

The Autism's Got Talent show had put me on something of a high because it wasn't really about the performance. It was the feeling of joining a community that accepted me – the real me, as I am, the person behind the mask. I also felt I was doing something valuable for that community. Putting myself out there as a woman on the autism spectrum and showing what people like us could achieve with our dogs. And, on a personal level, Anna Kennedy had been, and continues to be, amazing – she is a true inspiration.

Later that year came another joy. My daughter Scarlett got married that November, to her partner Jesse, and I was able to travel down to Cornwall to be there, something I could never have done without Kratu – family occasions had always been my bête noire and this was a *big* family occasion.

To watch the ceremony and see Scarlett exchanging her wedding vows was amazing. I was just so incredibly proud of her. She was such a wonderful mother and I was sure she would be an equally wonderful wife. I was already witnessing how, with her own little boy, Oscar, she was such a natural mother, able to do effortlessly all the things I had so struggled with. To see her happy truly made my heart smile. It was also wonderful to have Kratu as part of it. He had charmed the registrar sufficiently that she let him take pole position next to her for the entire ceremony. I had also made a flower garland for Scarlett and Jesse's dog, Bonnie, colour co-ordinated with Polo's blue eyes. The photos are beautiful and my eyes still well up every time I look at them.

As usual, the trip was not without a Kratu-related incident. I was being driven down by my friend Emma and we'd rented a cottage, so I'd packed a few provisions for our stay. Before I'd even set off to Emma's, Kratu had unpacked my travel bag, found and opened a packet of truffle salami and eaten the whole thing, leaving the empty packet in the middle of the sitting room. I found him smacking his lips, clearly pleased with his premier detective skills. The giant dog treat had obviously been his reward. Great, I thought, truffle farts for the entire journey.

Not to be out-master-criminalled by his brother, Polo joined in for the return trip, for which I'd cooked a packet of organic beef sausages from the local farm shop in the village. The pilfering pair almost snaffled the lot of them. I managed to grab one and defiantly ate it in front of them with great relish – and they were delicious sausages, I'll give them that.

After sunshine, almost inevitably comes rain. In late November 2019 I had another scare with Maia. She was twelve now and I was sure that her tumour had returned. It turned out it hadn't but it shook me to the core, bringing into focus once again that her time with us was finite.

Then, just as the year was coming to a close, I began to notice something very slightly off in the way Kratu was walking. I wasn't sure if it was anything to worry about but I started watching him with an eagle eye, though I could hear more than see that there was some sort of problem: a slight scraping sound when we walked. To be honest it was so faint and intermittent that I thought I might be imagining it, but no, my supersonic autistic hearing was having none of it. Something was not right.

So, to be on the safe side, I took him to see my vet, where he had an ultrasound scan. After that, I hoped it wouldn't be anything sinister, but the vet told me he couldn't confirm what the problem was with any certainty, so recommended I see a specialist and perhaps get an MRI scan to see if it would shed more light on the problem.

Which left me with another problem because I knew Kratu would have to go into the procedure alone, normal practice at most places being that you simply hand your dog over and leave the professionals to take them to theatre and sedate them. I couldn't do this because I knew Kratu wouldn't readily accept it. He'd get too stressed and end up having to be muzzled, perhaps even physically restrained, which could so easily bring about the mistrust of strangers I'd spent his whole life working hard not to invoke.

Obviously, as he was a therapy dog, I couldn't risk this happening anyway, but it was more than that – his whole life had been one of positivity and kindness and I didn't want to risk his good nature. Work had to be done to find a place with the very best experts and who would also allow me to be with him during sedation and then again back with him in recovery.

I understood the scale of the task; just as over-anxious parents can instil added anxiety in their children, veterinary practices don't want neurotic owners making things worse by transmitting their anxiety to their pets. And I got that. It was just that no one had ever handled Kratu apart from me and these breeds are not easy to manage if they get upset. I researched hard, eventually finding a clinic in Surrey who'd allow me to stay with Kratu during sedation and recovery.

But even with that major anxiety off my list, I was still overwhelmed and by the day of Kratu's appointment, knowing how serious things *could* be, my world was beginning to cave in. I just couldn't imagine my life without him. He was still a young dog and there was so much life still to be lived together. Fear was sitting heavily in my stomach and I was grateful beyond words that Penel Malby (photographer of *Dogs Today*, and by now a good friend) came along to support me.

My consultant was Dr Rodolfo Cappello DVM, PhD, DipECVN, MRCVS, a European Specialist in Veterinary Neurology & Neurosurgery, with, as you can see, a reassuring number of letters after his name. Still, on 2 December at noon, my mind refused to be reassured and the consultant's expression as Kratu walked for him and he examined him didn't do much to reassure me either.

Dr Cappello explained that he suspected it was a degenerating disc, which might be pressing on one of the nerves in Kratu's spine – something the MRI scan itself then confirmed. He had, to give its proper name, degenerative lumbosacral stenosis, which essentially meant his condition would worsen with age and he would be on pain medication for the rest of his life.

'There's an operation I could do now,' he added, 'which has a 95 per cent success rate.' But all I could see was the other number, the one he didn't say: that 5 per cent for whom the operation didn't work. For me this was particularly close to home as a dear friend had recently been in just that situation with a hip problem. Her dog had had the operation and it hadn't worked, which led to further operations and despite round-the-clock loving care over a period of several months, she ended up not only being one of those 5 per cent, but, tragically, losing her life as well. Could this be our fate? This was a possibility and reality. It was a wake-up call to the reality of surgery: there were no guarantees and I now had to call it.

I called it: we agreed that Dr Cappello would operate in January. But with the decision made, for better or worse, I still felt very wobbly. The thought of Kratu not being able to do the things he loved to do – running around crazily, jumping and leaping, zooming around, those handbrake turns of his ... He was a dog who manifested his joy in such powerful physical ways and the thought of him losing that broke my heart. Physicality was his very essence and if he was in that 5 per cent, he could be crippled for life. This was very unappetising food for thought.

In short, I felt defeated. It was as if life had kicked away my legs too. So what do you do then? You try to help someone else. There were people struggling everywhere, after all. And just as rescuing Kratu and liberating Tutty had brought me so much, I knew shifting my focus away from my own obstacles would mean doing good and feeling better too.

Back to social media, then, where I knew I'd find multiple requests for help of the kind Kratu and I could provide. Sure enough, my gaze was drawn to a primary school in Kent, where they were fundraising to support their most impoverished pupils – children for whom there wouldn't just be no Christmas presents, there would be little in the way of food and heating either.

Why does one thing grip your heart with such force over another? In this case it was because that situation was something I knew so well. I knew what it was like to have no food. I knew what it was like to be cold and homeless. I knew how that kind of despair felt. Christmas might be one big fuck-up for me after so many ones spent alone, destitute and with drug problems, all too aware of other families coming together, but innocent children deserved something better. It upset me a lot. So *do* something, I thought to myself. No one ever gets helped without effort.

And I knew this was something Kratu and I could help with. We could use our own social media profile to help the school raise money; we could share the campaign for them. And then I thought, *wait!* We could do a bit more than that, couldn't we? I still had treats and toys left over from various show winnings. Why didn't we drive down to Kent so the children could meet Kratu and donate those gifts to the school for the children who had pets? They surely had a greater need for those things.

My idea in place, I called the school and we made a plan: a surprise visit (the children were to know nothing about it), where I'd give them the donations and hopefully bring a little Kratu Christmas cheer.

Operation Bleak Midwinter was a go!

It was a long drive down to the school in Margate, but as ever, Kratu was in full singing kettle mode at the prospect of another adventure and equally thrilled to lap up the welcome – among children, he was always in his element. He entertained the children with some tricks and for their part, they were *amazing*; such a credit to their parents and such ambassadors for their school, which we toured with a group of lovely girls from Year 6, whom we dubbed 'Kratu's Angels' after Charlie's. And as we worked our way around the various classrooms (some of the teachers as astonished to see us as their pupils), it felt, every time I saw faces light up, as if Kratu was leaving a trail of stardust in his wake.

Smiles are great, of course, as are dog treats, but they can't fill children's bellies so it wasn't just about the visit itself. Our involvement also meant they smashed the school fundraising target and we could leave in the knowledge that Operation Bleak Midwinter would be in a position to help even more local children.

And it also helped me. Though I was never going to be someone who enjoyed Christmas, particularly this Christmas, I had remembered something valuable. That having a focus other than what was going on in my own life – a tool I already used often – could be beneficial to other people too.

They say facing your fears is a great way to overcome them, but when it came to putting Kratu through surgery, my fears were very real and firmly based on the practical as well as the emotional (I still couldn't stop thinking about that 5 per cent). I knew that recovery from surgery needed space and peace and warmth – three things I couldn't provide in my bungalow. A home full of big dogs with no central heating was the last place for a post-operative dog to recuperate, so shortly after the New Year, I called to cancel Kratu's surgery. Or at least postpone it until a later date. In the meantime, we would manage his condition more holistically, using my trusty Photizo red light therapy whenever I needed to, plus physio and restricting his wild ways. Which wasn't the easiest route, obviously. He would specialise in tearing off behind my back to do something dastardly, then get sore and make sure I knew all about it. Following this treatment plan, Kratu returned to his happy, healthy self. For me, it was the right path, balancing taking care of his condition medically with giving him the alternative treatments I believed in: we could revisit the prospect of surgery later.

Where All-party Parliamentary Dog Advisory Welfare Group (APDAWG) was concerned, however, the benefits of facing my fears had become abundantly apparent. We had attended our second meeting the previous autumn (concerned with greater regulation in dog training) and by the time of the third meeting, in January 2020, I was actually looking forward to going down to London to catch up with everyone in the way I assumed 'normal' people did.

APDAWG meetings are often themed and this was another gathering to celebrate an unsung hero. On this occasion it was an incredible woman called Eileen Jones, who runs a small charity in Wales, doing vital work helping rescue and rehome dogs she has rescued from puppy farms – another 'industry' in urgent need of more scrutiny and legislation. She's also involved with the Welsh arm of Lucy's Law, the campaign set up by TV vet Marc Abraham which after ten years has been passed into law and bans the for-profit third-party trade in puppies and kittens.

Animals know, they really do, when they are among friends. By now, everyone knew Kratu and as soon as he entered the room you could immediately feel this great whoosh of love as everyone gathered round for their turn in his happy orbit. And what an honour to be again in such illustrious company, among some of the great names in animal welfare who worked so tirelessly to achieve what they do. Peter Egan, Pen Farthing, Lisa Cameron MP, the glamorous and beautiful K-9 Angels, Marc the vet (who was awarded an OBE in the Queen's Birthday Honours of 2021) and Donna McDonald, a tireless campaigner hoping to make the pet industry 100 per cent cruelty-free.

That these people even exist is a blessing in itself, but to find myself among them, to be accepted as *one* of them, to be able to count some of them as friends ... Needless to say, I find it hard to put my feelings about that into words.

It was the sense of true belonging and being among people I'd always felt apart from, something it had taken half a lifetime to genuinely feel. To be part of something that did so much good, something I so respected, was one of the greatest gifts of all.

CHAPTER 25

A Freestyle Farewell

Crufts number four was coming up and that year Wendy suggested that Polo join the Wood Green team instead of Kratu. He was still so young and had done so well in Agility training; this would be an important step on his own journey.

I felt so sad, though. And not for me. For poor Kratu, who I knew would be beyond miffed to be usurped in such a way. Just the thought of setting off for Birmingham without him was almost too upsetting to contemplate, even though I completely respected Wendy's decision.

The more I thought about it, the more I realised that if I did go without him, I would not be able to walk through the door when I got home. He would smell the smells on me – of the people, of the dogs and of a place he loved. It would feel as if I was being disloyal. You will not be surprised to hear that a plan was quickly born. Because why couldn't Kratu go too? It would be perfect. He was in fine form and this would not be too taxing: a quick hello, goodbye tunnel and a lovely gentle sedate retirement run goodbye.

But with less of the run bit – he could manage that quite easily without compromising himself.

I immediately emailed Sara Wilde at the Kennel Club, asking if Kratu could do a 'retirement' run instead, and her reply lifted my spirits immensely. 'What might be nice,' she suggested, 'is after Oli runs his final round and his announcement is made, Kratu then gets to have one last time in the tunnel and Nathalie [one of the organisers, from another of the rescue dog charities] can build this into the commentary that Kratu is retiring as well. How does that sound?'

Oli, the fellow retiree, was a Jack Russell Terrier who had also been in a rescue team and had performed at Crufts for the last few years. For Kratu and I to go on after him would be perfect. I emailed back to thank her.

Mission accomplished once again!

Well, *one* mission. There was still the business of training Polo, but as he was so naturally smart and enjoyed it all so much, I didn't have any worries on that score. He was becoming quite accomplished in his own right now. Kratu, on the other hand, found it all a huge joke, would steal toys and run off to the tunnel, then hide in there, squeaking them with a furious intensity. It made me laugh and I allowed it; I had decided Kratu knew best about his freestyle agility and let him dance to the beat of his own drum. Let him be happy, I thought. After all, it made me happy and so many others too. I also found it hilarious and I know my laughter was what marked the behaviour for him: laughter as a reward rather than treats worked so well.

Kratu's final Crufts appearance in March 2020 didn't start terribly well. Though the day had begun okay, I hit a roadblock when Wendy went off to see the heads of the other teams and returned with the news that there'd been a change of plan. Oli, not Kratu, would be going on last; Kratu would be asked to go on before him, at the end of the Wood Green team's last performance of the session.

This change mattered to me so when it sunk in something snapped in me and I proceeded to have a meltdown. I understand why *now* – it's never good to change the goalposts with an autistic person, especially when they are already in the middle of a sensory overload. But at the time I was simply furious and dropped several F-bombs and hurled them around to the consternation of everyone around me. Which included Wendy, who had never seen me like this before, and my Facebook friend Sarah, whom I'd only just met in person, and who had come along specifically to handle Polo for me.

To their eternal credit, both were amazing. Neither batted an eyelid at my outburst and Wendy hurried off, saying, 'Leave it with me!'

I don't know what she did or said, but incredibly she returned a couple of minutes later to let me know that the order had been changed back again.

I calmed down just enough to go and do my round with Polo, who, after an unsettled start (my fault entirely – I was just so shaken), went on to do a really good course. It didn't go unnoticed. Sarah and Kratu, who were in the waiting arena, watched the whole thing on screen, Kratu not taking his eyes off me and Polo for a moment. And by the time it was *his* turn in the spotlight, there was no question that he was very, very cross with me. Stinker Polo going on before him? That just wasn't how it worked.

So now we were both in a mood. I was miffed. He was miffed. Nothing for it, then: we'd give the audience a bit of freestyle rebellion and mayhem, both things that went with Kratu hand in paw. So I willed him to get out there and do exactly what he wanted and my goodness, he took me at my word. We walked into the middle and he went bounding off with glee, straight into the tunnel to do his now-signature switch, then a quick lie-down, and out and run off again. Sensing the crowd's appreciation, he then took himself off round the arena once more, just loving the whole atmosphere, just loving performing. He swerved a couple of jumps, did an inspection of the perimeter and more tunnel manoeuvres, then, without warning, instead of doing one jump he simply picked up the end of the pole in his teeth and went bounding off across the arena with it. *I've stolen the pole!* he seemed to be saying. *It's mine now and I'm running away with it!* The audience were roaring.

He then headed back to the tunnel and dropped the pole at the entrance (though I suspect he'd have taken it in with him if he could) and, obviously so excited by this rascal act of ingenuity, he then got a bit of a zoomie on … Back and forth he flew, soaking up the crowd's appreciation. Almost everyone was on their feet now and his whole body responded, as if to say, 'How about *that? Come on, I* owned *it!*' The other dogs were already coming through for the final parade round but Kratu didn't care – he was just so damned pleased with himself.

He had come, he had seen, he had performed like a star. The commentators remarked that they had saved the best till last: he had gone out in true style, in his own Kratu style. Now *that's* how you do a final performance.

As before, the media went mad for Kratu's antics and though I was getting used to it all by now, it was still an intense couple of days.

As well as all sorts of requests from across the world about him, I was deluged by tweets and messages on social media. If someone likes Kratu and comments, I want to respond – it's only polite, after all – so I went into robot mode for the first forty-eight hours, spending long stints at my laptop, becoming Kratu essentially and interacting with his fans around the world. By the beginning of the next week, I was completely shattered.

And it didn't stop there. On the Monday I was asked to do a live interview for a Canadian TV news programme, which ended up, because of the time difference, being really late at night. Kratu slept through the whole thing, only waking up briefly for a few treats.

Then on Tuesday, I got an email from the production office of Kay Burley's Sky News programme. Would I like to bring Kratu to their studios that Thursday to do a live interview about his performance?

I knew Kratu would like that, would like it very much indeed, in fact, so I emailed back immediately, saying yes please, even though I knew it would mean a ridiculously early start. I was at last beginning to find my feet at such times; grounded by Kratu's paws, I was even beginning to enjoy them, finding that the camera – so impersonal, and so different to a human face – held little or no fear. I called on my Prussian ancestors for the necessary planning to pull this off; my week was fast turning into a military manoeuvre.

But then came something that blew me almost right into the stratosphere. I was just looking at train times for the Sky News gig when a message arrived. A direct personal message, on Twitter. It was from Marc Abraham:

Hey, would Kratu like to be APDAWG's canine ambassador?
☺☺ x

It was just as well Marc hadn't phoned me because tears welled in my eyes and, frankly, I was speechless. This had come completely out of the blue. I had always struggled to see the good in things, to be positive and optimistic. To ignore the voice that had haunted me since childhood: *you're an outsider, you're worthless, whatever you might think or do, you're still no good.* I was, and in some ways still am, a classic misfit. Because of my random, unpredictable and sometimes inappropriate behaviour, I was always on the outside, looking in. Lost and hurting, screaming out for answers, just desperate to be heard. Why, oh why, had I been born with the sort of complicated shape that didn't seem to fit into *any* kind of hole?

Being accepted without judgement in this way was a huge deal for me. Marc had opened a new door by allowing me to attend those APDAWG meetings. It had become a place where I felt I belonged. We all shared the same interests – animal welfare, making changes, supporting those changes – all doing the very best we could to give dogs a voice. So for Kratu to be asked to be a canine ambassador was no less than epic. I thought back to when I'd first met Marc and Peter at Pup Aid, me in a meltdown, in the show ring, unable to articulate myself properly … to now. Being part of something that meant so much to me. Being able to talk without fear paralysing my brain. Being able to relax, to be heard.

To feel I was among friends.

We had worked so hard, Kratu and me, and finally, us two underdogs had fitted in. We had been seen, taken seriously and accepted.

It was a moment, and a day, like no other. I felt pride, of course, overwhelming pride in my boy from the camp. My best friend, my soulmate, my incredible Kratu. And such a huge sense of worth and achievement, it made my heart swell with joy. But it made me feel something else as well: with Kratu, I had learned to identify and understand what love was. And now another emotion too.

It was happiness.

Epilogue

September 2021

Kratu has had to slow up recently. He gets more pain when he does zoomies after Polo.

I watch him.

I see how light he is on that back leg. I see his back flinch slightly. I see his limp when I haven't stopped him in time from jumping up on something he shouldn't.

I have to step up my care, as I want to delay the inevitable surgery until it is absolutely necessary. I don't want to take the chance before then that he could become paralysed as a result of the procedure going wrong.

Yesterday, as I finished writing this book, he was lying on the grass with a ball in his mouth, squishing it rhythmically, lost in his own Kratu world, and I thought I would like a photo of his eye with me reflected in it.

So I leant over him and I saw me, reflected in his eye. The huge wave of love for him hit me so hard – I didn't know it was coming, this feeling that my heart, full to capacity, was now overflowing, streaming, flooding my body and through my eyes, tears dripping to the ground. I never had any idea how huge love could be. How beautiful it was.

Now I realised. This is it. Love. Moving, flowing, it is HUGE! It is a powerful, gentle, almost sparkly, effervescent sense of light in motion.

I lay down next to him. He and I together, our gazes so deeply entwined, such a powerful force.

He put a paw forward, covering my hand, and I held it oh, so gently.

Yes, my love. We have come a long way together. And we still have a way to go yet.

We lay on the grass together then and our souls smiled.

Sometimes something is right, sometimes magic is real. For me, Tess, who by rights should not have been here, who had not just been broken, but smashed up by life. Not only that, I have found love. Well, it has found me. It is something so special and beautiful that it could not be contained. Kratu is a force of nature whose spirit and happiness cannot be contained. He *is* magic. He is the something right in my life.

I have become his guardian now. When the others go to the car, he waits patiently in the sitting room for me to come for him. He won't move. I stroke his head, our gazes locked into each other, and tell him how I love him so. He sighs then looks at me and signals, *Carry on. More ...*

So I sing him the songs of the ancient Transylvanians, the bears, the wolves, the mountains ... He then follows me out to the car, ready for adventures.

For Kratu, life is *always* an adventure. When he has a plan, nothing comes between him and his shenanigans, and his repertoire of skills continues to amaze me. Just lately, he's become something of an artist. A 3D specialist and very much the Banksy of the sculpture world (or so he thinks, anyway). I came home just a few days ago to a quite magnificent artistic display and crime scene. Two packets of basmati rice sprinkled around the sitting room, arranged with an expensive brand of Italian linguini, topped with a drizzle of extra virgin olive oil from the carefully rearranged and emptied sardine tins that had been made into the *pièce de résistance* on top.

Not everything, however, had been used. The easy-to-open boxes of boring everyday food had all been left intact as they were clearly not of the required standard for this masterpiece.

Do I need to name the artist or the villain? I wondered aloud. Who could it be?

Only one dog is capable of such dastardly and cunning plotting and plans.

Professor Kratu Moriarty had been at it again.

Repetition and autism go hand in hand, as does learning lessons in life, not taking them on board and repeatedly making the same mistakes. This is especially true with toxic relationships. I gave up on trying in the human world; I've been on my own for many years now and happily so.

Until Kratu, that is. People talk about their soulmate, their twin flame and so on. My heart's biggest yearning and desire was to be accepted for who I am and to be loved unconditionally. It was very hard to process that love came in a canine form, but it was also the most liberating truth.

Yes, I truly had found what most people spend their lives

searching for but first I had to let go of the limiting belief that maybe there was a human someone waiting for me when, in fact, I already had everything I needed in Kratu.

To see a diamond in your hand, covered in dirt, and to throw it away because it's mucky is pure and utter folly. Instead, take the time to clean it and polish the surface. When you hold it up in the sunlight, you will see the light cascade and sparkle all around you.

What I have is the most precious gift I could ever have imagined and for the most part, I thought I was not worthy of it. So back to repetition, and calling in those life moments that can teach you or guide you instead of the painful ones that had dominated my life. I was now, after all the self-work and changing my perceptions, experiencing happy ones too.

I had not thought it possible, considering how deep our bond and connection already were, but Kratu and I have reached a new place. One of the blocks I found hardest to overcome was touch. I gave up trying partly because of my natural autistic avoidance but mostly because of painful associated memories.

Especially at night. As I explained very early on in this book, one of my PTSD waking nightmares is to feel the bed go down as if someone is climbing in next to me. I freeze with fear, my heart pounds and I break into a cold sweat. I want to scream – help, help, help! – but I have lost my voice. My scream is silent, my lips cannot move. The memories hit me hard in an avalanche of abuse. I lie there, shocked. How could this have happened? How could I have survived? Why me?

And then the fear of being touched hits me harder still – now a waking, conscious, terrifying experience.

I need to stop it, to dig deep. Then something new appears … I hear breathing. But not in the nightmare. Outside it … Through that fog of fear and terror I can hear a little huffle-puff breathing.

The swirling fog recedes back into the dark place it came from.

Then I hear a snuffle and my consciousness changes. And I can move. I slide my arm out to the side of the bed and touch warm fur. I hear Kratu, I feel him. Grounded back into reality, into safety, I practise gratitude and thank every single thing I can think of. The sun, the moon, the stars, the cosmos, trees and nature ... Then drift back into a bizarre sleep of colourful dreams.

In my strange world of broken sleep, I now wake to find Kratu back to back with me. In a deep slumber. Joined at the hip. He is there: not on his bed, but mine. Right next to me. His presence wards off the night demons. They do not come as often now, but I can manage much better when they do.

I said good morning the other day and I held him. He lay happily in my arms and I held him there, happy too. Me, who struggles so greatly with touching and being touched. He turned his head and looked directly into my eyes, into my soul, just as I had held him in the very beginning. There *is* no beginning. No end. Just a circle. The *Ouroboros*, the never-ending circle, came back to mind. The *Ouroboros* has been said to mean infinity or wholeness. Rebirth, the integration of one's shadow.

Those lessons are now learned for me, self-acceptance and being able to accept touch being the two hardest to overcome. Now it's time to let them go as it is no longer relevant in my life.

The chapters are finished, I close the book on the past.

Kratu and I have a lot of life to live and enjoy each day, as fully present as we can possibly be. Whoever would have thought my little grey puppy from the Roma camp would have been my greatest

INCREDIBLE KRATU

teacher, my biggest support and the one who blew the clouds away
and let the sun shine again?

He did what mental health teams, psychiatrists and psychologists
could not do. What medication and therapy could not do for me
either. He guided me, taught me, allowed me to let go and heal
myself.

He loved and loves me, for who I was and am, unconditionally
accepting all of me without judgement.

I am his Tess and he is my Kratu.

Incredible.

Afterword

by Philip Tedeschi

This is a love story. Like every good love story, the basis for this meeting of the hearts best occurs by knowing one another deeply, with trust, communication and commitment. The uniquely sensitive and intuitive human–canine bond described in this work reveals a secret that can be difficult to capture in words. This heart-warming story reveals a simple and yet inspired insight into what it means to be connected, seen and how love changes the way we experience the world around us. This human–canine story of connection leans towards magic and happy endings ... a meeting destined to last a lifetime. This real-life 'it was meant to be' story illuminates the unique capacity that dogs have to accept us for exactly who we are and create a space for our most authentic selves to be nurtured. In the simplest terms, to feel loved for who we are. *Incredible Kratu* offers an unforgettable glimpse into the heart and soul of love.

Dr Philip Tedeschi
Executive Director, Institute for Human-Animal Connection,
University of Denver Graduate School of Social Work
June 2021

Acknowledgements

This has been a long journey; it's taken me out of the dark to Kratu, who's helped me find myself and unconditional love.

My motivation for writing this book was that hopefully I will help others by telling my story. Maybe other people can learn how to let go of heavy stuff, find the lighter energies and reconnect with themselves, embracing a much happier way of being. Going through the system, being diagnosed with multiple labels, struggling with the lack of support and help available left me only one choice: to dig deep, find the strength and the belief systems that resonated and then to do the self-work needed to be empowered and free. Finding a purpose through Kratu allowed me to see the world differently; through Kratu's eyes of joy and love, as he became my clarity, focus and guidance. I hope that those who need it will find the strength to do the same.

Then there is a need to tell the truth. The motivation behind dog rescue is often about money and not the dogs' welfare and because of this too many dogs who come to the UK, like Kratu, have to be returned to rescue. This needs to change. Rescue dogs require rehabilitation, training and their needs understood and met, especially those with traumatic pasts. However, too often people are unaware of what they are taking on and what is needed, which frequently leads to the dogs being misunderstood and mishandled. It is crucial for people to understand more about training and the dogs themselves, so I encourage everyone considering adopting a rescue to make the effort; research, educate yourself, reap the rewards. Dogs are family and for life.

There are so many people who have been a part of my and Kratu's story, but my especial thanks to the following people, without whom, our journey to this finished book could not have happened. To Lynne Barrett-Lee and the buzzards, thank you to them, for bringing us together, and to Lynne, for your Tigger presence to my Eyore, for holding little Tess's hand when big Tess had melted down and disappeared. This has been such a wonderful journey with you, your patience and smiles throughout have been so special. To Andrew Lownie, for taking me onboard and your acceptance of me. And to Ellie Carr and all the team at Bonnier for seeing Kratu's light and offering us the chance to write this book. I'm forever truly grateful to you for making a dream come true, for believing in us and giving us this opportunity. I cannot thank you enough and I am grateful for everyone's help in making this book come to life.

To all the journalists, producers and photographers at newspapers, magazines, news channels and TV programmes – thank you! You made him go viral. You sent Kratu worldwide. Big thank you to Sky News and Kay Burley; Ethan Marrell aka Ozzyman Reviews for the hilarious and unforgettable reviews; Special mention to Beverley Cuddy and *Dogs Today*; Michelle Machin-Jefferies; Penel Malby, for judging that fateful day at Dog Fest raising the bar for what we could achieve and your brilliant cover photo for *Dogs Today* magazine; *Your Dog* Magazine for our first cover; Dion Gallichan Photography, for your cover photo and kindness;

Julia Claxton Photography for your outstanding Pup Aid photos; Natasha Balletta photography for wonderful Crufts photos, adventures and friendship; Warren photographic Ltd for *Your Dog* cover photo; Wolfhound Photography; award-winning Little Pip Photography; lastly to Michelle Linaker and all those involved at the Daily Mirror People's Pet Awards, for recognising the worldwide love for Kratu, then creating his own category and Social Media Superstar award!

To the supporters of both Kratu and myself, I am hugely thankful. Sophi Stewart, for the gift of Maia the wolfy one, who was to lead me out of the iniquitous den of darkness that was my old life. For agreeing to take on Hero and Simi. And for being my dear and wonderful friend who went the distance with me and never gave up on me; Peter Egan and Marc Abrahams, both of you were there at the start of our journey, then throughout, and your presence helped to inspire us; Maria Slough for helping us attend the European Parliament film screening and Dominic Dyer for support and friendship; Kim Webb a dear kind friend and a special dedication to your beloved Millie; Suzanne Martin, Karen Nicholson, Sally Marchant, Georgette, all dear friends and your support is so appreciated. You have been invaluable through this last year of great difficulty for me; also thanks to Angie Chocolate, Kay Hollier, Lisa Hatley, Karen Chamberlain, you're all friends who help so much; Hilary Hornby, your help kept them all together; Ergun you are a family pack member; Donna Macdonald, for believing in me, inspiring and encouraging me along the way; Celia Blacu none of this would have happened without you, you changed our lives; Helen Fentem-Jones, our superb physio; Sarah Beddington, for being a constant source of unfailing support; and finally to Dr Colm Magee, without the diagnosis my life would have been too hard to navigate and the happiness I found unachievable.

Crufts and The Kennel Club, Sara Wilde, for all your special shows where Kratu performed his finest routines; Wood Green Animal Charity, thank you for having the facility and behavior team that enables other people like me to keep dogs in their homes; to Wendy Kruger, thank you, my teacher. I can never thank you enough for all the classes and the invite into the rescue dog agility team, the result was unexpected; Anna Kennedy for accepting us into your charity as Ambassadors, your huge support and for AGT – the first dog comedy routine; Philip Tedeschi, for your beautiful words summarising that love connection and bond Kratu and I share; Andrew Hale and Dr Daniel Mills for helping with dog wisdom and knowledge; Sara Kinge and all the team at Natural Instinct for their sponsorship, food of my champions! Raffy could stay with us because of your support; Andy Little at Active dogs for your supplements; Photizo and Ruth, we love our Photizo vet care; Lida vets and Ilan for working with us; Jo Amit for your kindness; Wetnose Animal Aid for inviting us to be Ambassadors; in loving memory of Jude, who founded and ran Friends of Animals in Need who helped me adopt my wonderful Paqo.

And finally, to my family. To my daughter Scarlett. I am so proud of you and all you have become. You are a wonderful mother. I know I never was, but I feel I did something right in your life, as you are so grounded, kind, balanced and a truly amazing, beautiful woman. To dear Caspar, I wish you all the strength you need to dig deep enough inside to find your own way and happiness. And to my mum, I hope you see that I actually did something you will deem as good in my life. I hope that makes you happy.

And most importantly, to all who have seen Kratu, met Kratu, smiled because of him, had their spirits lifted because of him and laughed because of him. To all those connections around the world, thank you. Kratu was destined to shine a light and he does that brightly. You all shine your own beautiful lights too, and your presence is so very welcome. You are all very special to us.

Love always, Tess and Kratu

© David Bell